"Sal is a genius at recognizing the potential in a committed writer. He speaks with the authority of one who whose knowledge of publishing pertains to every type of book. With patience and dry humor, Sal encourages writers to express their ideas in their own voice, and guides the new writer through the terrifying world of publishing. I couldn't have written my first book without him. He's already promised to stick with me through the next."

CYNTHIA L. WALL, LCSW,
AUTHOR OF *The Courage to Trust: a guide to deep and lasting relationships* AND *Embracing True Prosperity* (AUDIOTAPE)

"Sal Glynn brings levity as only an insider with a sense of humor can to the heart-attack seriousness with which most of us writers approach the business of getting published. A must-have for writers serious about seeing their words in print."

MARTHA ALDERSON,
AUTHOR OF *Blockbuster Plots Pure & Simple*

"I will be recommending your delightfully honest little book and giving copies as gifts to young writers who I've worked with over the years as their story midwife."

DAVID WEITZMAN,
AUTHOR OF *Rama and Sita,* AND *A Subway for New York*

The Dog Walked Down the Street

*An Outspoken Guide for
Writers Who Want to Publish*

Sal Glynn

Cypress House
Fort Bragg, California

THE DOG WALKED DOWN THE STREET
An Outspoken Guide for Writers Who Want to Publish
Copyright © 2006 by Sal Glynn.

CYPRESS HOUSE
155 Cypress Street
Fort Bragg, CA 95437
www.cypresshouse.com
800-773-7782

Cover design and book production by Cypress House
Typeset in Monotype Bembo

Cover photograph © GambiCats Charity, used by permission. GambiCats started working with stray and feral cats in The Gambia, West Africa, in 1998 and became a UK Registered Charity in 1999. They now also work with stray and feral dogs. For more information, please visit www.gambicats.org.uk or e-mail gambicats@aol.com.

EXCERPTS USED BY PERMISSION

Between Time and Timbuktu by Kurt Vonnegut, Jr., Random House / Bantam Dell Publishing Group.

One Step Behind: A Kurt Wallander Mystery © 2002 by Henning Mankell (The New Press).

LIBRARY OF CONGRESS CATALOGING IN PUBLICATION DATA
Glynn, sal, 1955-
   The dog walked down the street : an outspoken guide for writers who want to publish / sal glynn.
      P. Cm.
   Isbn-13: 978-1-879384-66-8 (pbk. : Alk. Paper)
   1. Authorship--marketing. 2. Book proposals. I. Title.
   Pn161.G58 2006
   070.5'2--Dc22

                                             2006004919

PRINTED IN CANADA

10 9 8 7 6 5 4 3 2 1

Most poets...can't even write a simple line like,
"The dog walked down the street."

CHARLES BUKOWSKI

ACKNOWLEDGMENTS

A WAVE OF THE BLUE PENCIL to Jan Campbell, who introduced me to the editor's way while knocking a bit of yellow journalism, "The Queen's Tour Makes Us Puke," into reasonable shape.

SPECIAL THANKS ARE DUE to the fine people who read and commented on various drafts of *The Dog*: Cynthia Frank, Brian Peterson, Joe Shaw, Nancy Ellis, Brook Barnum, Linda Pack, Theresa Whitehill, Rebecca Woolf, Caroline and Jürg Weber, Kate Erickson, Douglas Moore, and George Young. Most of them come from good homes.

FOREWORD

THERE IS QUITE A DIFFERENCE between a sapling and a grown tree, but only time separates them, time and growth and a committed caretaker, and several seasons of leaves. I met Sal Glynn at the Big Sur Fiction Writer's workshop in the spring of 2004, when my novel was a flimsy sapling with a few leaves awkwardly sticking up like hair-plugs and twigs for arms. I had started the first draft and was in search of water, sunlight, and a whole lot of guidance. I liked Sal immediately. He spent the weekend surrounded by first-time authors who picked his brain and scribbled notes on their arms and spiral notebooks while he puffed on Swiss cigarettes. I waited for the right time to bum one of his Française and make friends.

Before meeting Sal I thought of an editor as sitting at a desk with a blue pencil and a green celluloid eyeshade. They were the punctuation police who inserted commas in run-on sentences, Strunk and White bible in hand.

Sal explained over dim sum that he considered himself a book midwife instead of an editor. Had I heard him correctly? The surrounding patrons were listening in on our conversation, their expressions puzzled. Not every day did two respectable people relate midwifery to manuscripts over seaweed salad.

"I deliver books!"

"Sounds cool. Can you deliver mine?"

The first draft of my novel left me overwhelmed by the work ahead. The draft was like coughing, words scattered everywhere like seeds. I thumbed through my pages somewhat lost. There were too many questions in need of an outside perspective by someone who believed in my work and believed I could write better.

"Tell me what you are trying to do," he said.

"I'm trying to hold the characters together with a story."

"You will need a lot of glue."

Starting a manuscript is like getting married to a complete stranger or jumping into a pool of sharks. Who is to know if they are the man-eating kind? For two years Sal stood by my side. Draft after draft, he studied my novel, held my hand during temper tantrums, and distracted me from mental breakdowns with hard laughs. He taught me how to pluck weeds by the root, and trim branches when they grew out of control. He was attentive and nurturing and committed to my characters. "Just part of the job," Sal explained with mud in his fingernails. He made sure my story had the proper sunshine and shade.

No writer has the tools to write and publish a manuscript without guidance. We can only go so far on instinct. As writers we do not know what we are getting ourselves into when we set out to write a story. Even more, we do not know what we are getting ourselves into when we set off to sell one. Through the madness, joy and pain, and drafts of drafts, it is easy for one to get lost. A book midwife makes his mission to pick you up and brush you off.

The next best thing to calling Sal at 3 AM on a Tuesday night is thumbing through *The Dog Walked Down the Street*, a book of water, sun, and dirty fingernails.

May your pages grow strong.

Rebecca Woolf
August 2006

Rebecca Woolf is a former contributor to the *Chicken Soup for the Teenage Soul* series, novelist, masculist, and proud mom of Archer. She recounts her adventures in motherhood at www.girls gonechild.blogspot.com.

CONTENTS

INTRODUCTION   1

ARE YOU SURE? WELCOME TO PUBLISHING   5

THE FUN BEGINS: AGENTS, PROPOSALS, INQUIRY LETTERS   7

CONTRACT SHUFFLE WITH AGENTS AND PUBLISHERS   13

FRESH HOPE FOR A FIRST DRAFT   21

A HEALTHY WRITER IS A WRITING WRITER   33

HOW TO WORK WITH AN IN-HOUSE EDITOR   37

REWRITING AND THE WORD-WATCH LIST   40

FINAL MANUSCRIPT   47

TELLING A BOOK BY ITS COVER   52

COUNTDOWN TO THE END   57

CHECKING THE GALLEYS   61

ETHICAL COMMISERATION   63

AFTERMATH AND WRITERS SELLING THEIR BOOKS   67

ANNOTATED RESOURCE LIST   73

ABOUT THE WRITER   82

INTRODUCTION

BOOKS ARE WONDERFUL. They teach, question, entertain, and encourage us to dream. Given the choice between buying books and replacing an old pair of shoes that leak when it rains, I'll take the books. Shoes have never made me laugh at two in the morning. Even more wonderful than books are the people who write and want to write them.

Writing a book is hard and lonely, and anyone dedicated to the craft needs all the help they can get. Few non-writers understand the difficulties in presenting an argument or telling a story. Smart writers will hire a freelance editor who does more than check for spelling mistakes and this is where I come in. After having survived different-sized publishers as in-house editor, I decided to go where the fun has not stopped and work independently alongside writers as a book midwife. "Book doctor" sounds like pre-Semmelweiss surgery in a murky office, with hunchbacked Igor polishing the scalpels on his dirty apron. I prefer "book midwife." When the writer has the content and drive, the book midwife is ready with hot water and clean towels to help the pages come out, whether fiction, memoir, humor, self-help, business, cooking, health, or even coloring books. A book midwife provides support and encouragement for first-time and seasoned writers to be their best. They meet, telephone, and e-mail at any hour until the book is done. Nine to five is not enough time for writers, especially when on deadline.

Besides the necessary handholding and mollycoddling, the book midwife also serves as tough critic. A harsh critic says, "This stinks," while a tough critic says, "Tell me what you are trying to do." Part of the job is citing rules of composition and structure. These are used the same as a runner's starting blocks, a place to kick against to solve a particular problem. Whether fiction or nonfiction, the story will tell the writer the rules to toss or follow. Devotion to Strunk and White does not produce a compelling manuscript.

Another of the book midwife's responsibilities is showing the writer how the publishing business works. According to an impossible to authenticate survey in 2002, 81 percent of Americans think they have the material to knock out a book if they had the spare time. It ain't that easy. If they knew what was involved, the figure would be knocked down to 8.1 percent. There are proposals and pitch letters to agents, outlines and synopses, and successive drafts leading to the final manuscript. When a publisher accepts the book, try being heard above the noise of the 175,000 new books clacking off the presses every year.

Publishing has changed greatly since the days of the gentleman's profession. Judith Regan, with her own imprint at HarperCollins, said this in *The New York Times* about present-day challenges in publishing: "It's all become a big, fat, screaming, mean, vicious, greedy, rude and crude fest." The corporate environment has in-house editors spending more time with deals and marketing meetings than manuscripts. Editing and developing new writers has shifted to agents and freelance editors, who give them the attention few publishers can offer.

The trade burns out people through long hours and low pay, and squabbles over profit margins and advertising budgets. Those who stay in the business for longer than ten years are there for the books. One veteran editor explained working in publishing by comparing it to a marriage. There is excitement at the big day, being hired or signing a contract, and romping through the honeymoon. Editor or writer and publisher learn to accommodate the other's likes and dislikes until the disenchantment begins. Who wants to write or make books anyway and who cares if they do? Years go by marked by fighting and counseling. Trial separations prove they are unsuited for other endeavors. The couple remains together against everyone else's better judgment. Bickering and blame are spread on the morning toast along with the margarine and marmalade.

Then the marvelous occurs. The editor or writer accepts they love what they do against all reason. She looks across the bed to the sleeping bulk of her spouse and pulls him close. He farts, a gentle whisper but still a fart. Big deal. The bed is warm, the rent is paid, and tomorrow is a new manuscript.

Based on answers to real questions asked by writers, *The Dog Walked Down the Street* is also part commonplace book. The *Oxford English Dictionary* has the term appearing in 1578. A commonplace book, or book of common places, is defined as "A book in which 'commonplaces' or passages important for reference were collected, usually under general heads; hence, a book in which one records passages or matters to be especially remembered or referred to, with or without arrangement."

The fancier autodidacts say "commonplace" is a translation of the Latin *locus communis*, meaning "a theme or argument of general application." Cheaper paper in the sixteenth century made the commonplace book possible. Stationers bound blank sheets and sold them as scrapbooks to be filled with proverbs, recipes, letters, weights and measures, and prayers. Readers and writers used commonplaces to help them remember what they had learned. There have been literary dandies among commonplace books, like those of John Milton, E. M. Forster, and Wallace Stevens. Contemporary writers keep commonplace books (they call them "journals" to avoid sounding like dusty antiquarians) at their sides to jot down quotes from what they are reading, and brief babbles about plot and character problems.

The Dog steps outside the strictures of a commonplace book with requested and uncalled-for advice on how books are really made. This is not the Stanford publishing course. The book midwife promises to hold nothing back. Take what you need and ignore the rest, except the high praise for your commitment to writing.

This hairy animal began when writer Cynthia Wall collected what I had said while we worked on her first book, *The Courage to Trust*, and sent the short manuscript to me as a thank-you gift. She had demanded reasons why I had ripped out excess adverbs, adjectives, and participle phrases from her early drafts. I told her. I knew she was a better writer than she did, and we wrote and rewrote until the manuscript said what she wanted in the clearest language possible.

At the same time Cynthia and I were finishing *Courage,* I started working with two fledgling novelists, Rebecca Woolf and Douglas Moore. They challenged me as I went through their manuscripts, and we had loads of fun and lots of conversations about fiction writing. Much of *The Dog* came from notebooks I started keeping after Cynthia Wall's first version. Noting writers' questions made it easier to give answers at conferences and also see where I was stumped.

Cynthia knew I was a better book midwife than I did, and encouraged me to add more material to her thank-you until we issued *The Dog* as a chapbook for the 2005 Mendocino Coast Writers Conference. Cynthia Frank, publisher of Cypress House, read the chapbook in manuscript and made an offer every book midwife dreams of—their very own book.

ARE YOU SURE?
WELCOME TO PUBLISHING

THE PUBLISHING OF BOOKS has a tradition spanning more than 500 years. Gutenberg drove himself into penury while printing his Bible from movable type, his lawyers foreclosing the mortgage on his shop and making off with the tools he developed. In Renaissance Venice, Aldus Manutius founded the first publishing firm, with editors and typesetters and printers concentrating on their different skills to put definitive Greek and Latin texts into the hands of hundreds of readers. For all of Aldus' high-minded standards, he also took on commissions for extra cash, like the classic confusion of the *Hypnerotomachia Poliphili*, beginning a parallel tradition of trying to make a living in this least remunerative of trades.

There have been seditious, libelous, and dangerous books that extended beyond their unassuming position on a shelf. Books have been accused of being demons or demon-inspired. They've been excoriated, banned, and, when needed, exorcised.

In the days when heretical books were burned, the fires were built on large stages. Despite the pains taken to demolish them, readable masses were found in the embers. The devil knew fire and its effects, and gave them his special protection. Juries found burning the heretics easier and less expensive.

Staunch royalist John Stubbs protested the proposed marriage of Queen Elizabeth with the Duke of Anjou, a bold act he committed in a work entitled *Discoveries of a Gaping Gulf whereinto England is like to be swallowed by another French marriage, if the Lord forbid not the banes by letting her Majestie see the sin and punishment thereof* (1579). Far from defaming the Virgin Queen, it was written with great affection, though pronounced "a fardel of false reports, suggestions, and manifest lies." The writer, along with the bookseller, was brought to the open market at Westminster, where their right hands were cut off with a butcher's knife and mallet. Taking his cap off with his left hand, Stubbs addressed the gathered crowd, shouting, "Long live Queen Elizabeth!"

In 1633, William Prynne published his *Histriomastix: The Player's Scourge*. In it he argued that stage plays were basically "sinful, heathenish, intolerable mischiefs to churches, to republics, to the manners, minds, and the souls of men." Since the king and queen both enjoyed dances and masques, the book and the writer were tried before the Star Chamber. Prynn's punishment was severe: he lost both his ears, was condemned to perpetual imprisonment, and fined 5,000 pounds. The book was ordered burned at the hand of the hangman.

Theodore Reinking, lamenting the diminished glory of his race, wrote a book entitled *Dania ad exteros de perfidia Suecorum* (1644). It was not an excellent work, and its writer a sloppy historian at best, but it aroused the anger of the Swedes, who cast Reinking into prison. Having sat for many years on the damp stones, he was offered his freedom on the condition that he lose his head or choose to eat his book. Preferring the gustatory alternative, the writer devoured his book after having cleverly converted it into a sauce.

The twenty-first century is different. Instead of worrying over being banned in Boston, a favorite in the 1950s, writers are faced with their books being ignored or remaindered. Publishers unload overstock to recyclers, where the covers are cut off and the pages pulped and bleached to appear again as your favorite toilet tissue. Yet there are those who persist in writing and publishing books. Here's to you.

THE FUN BEGINS:
AGENTS, PROPOSALS, INQUIRY LETTERS

EVERY WRITER NEEDS an agent to approach a publisher, and the weeks and months spent looking for the right one will make you happier, healthier, and more pleased with your final choice. A good agent is a member of the Association of Authors' Representatives, does not charge reading fees, promptly answers questions, and cares more for your career than for a quick advance. There are books about finding an agent (see annotate resource list), and the Web site www.first writer.com has a continually updated database of literary agents. *Talking Agents,* the newsletter of Agent Research and Evaluation (AR&E), is available online at www.agentresearch.com.

FOR NONFICTION WRITERS

WRITER: A publisher wants me to write a book about (insert subject).

BOOK MIDWIFE: Sounds good. Any money in it? Any for me?

Hungry, energetic, and aware in-house editors look at periodicals and Web sites for writers who have something interesting to say in a dynamic style. They contact the writer and ask for a manuscript, and the writer sends off a reasonable stack of paper. A check arrives, and six months later, the writer is inundated with media requests for interviews. The writer who breathes at sea level does not wait for this miracle, but works on a proposal.

A *proposal* includes title page, synopsis, list of contents, chapter outline, sample chapter, assessment of competition, and marketing plan. The complete package reflects the tone and flavor of the finished manuscript. If the proposal is on a humorous subject, let the weirdness roll. A stately, footnoted, and annotated serious work should be treated seriously. You're addressing people who want to know if the book can sell, not speaking to friends or defending a doctoral thesis.

When a writer recently appeared on a writer's panel in Baltimore, questions from the audience forced him to drain his hotel room's mini-bar. They wanted the secret of being published, as if he had clicked into the grand mystery. He tried to get the importance of content through their heads, then fled when a voice from the back row asked about film rights. The writer is recovering.

Start with the *synopsis*, no more than a page describing the manuscript in general terms. Write and rewrite it in clear declarative sentences until the damn thing has no extra words. Include why you are the expert suited to write this book. This is how your project will be perceived from now until publication date.

The *outline* is a breakdown of what goes where. Take books you admire and look at how the chapters, foreword, afterword, and citations are structured and used. Apply what you learn as a model to construct your outline. If other important issues and information appear while you're writing the final manuscript, you can make changes without anyone getting testy.

The *sample chapter* must be your absolutely best writing: twenty pages of sharp, clear, direct speech that talks with readers, not at or to them. Check your facts and check them again. If you're unsure of anything, leave it out.

Everything is going to be fine.

Selling your book is not selling out. Marketing is a major part of publishing. The number of new books published in this country each year wavers between staggering and frightening. Your *marketing plan* has to show the prospective publisher an audience and how to reach it. Saying that a book can be sold in brick-

and-mortar stores is weak. Too many titles are fighting for the limited shelf space. How much commitment are you willing to put into marketing the book? In-house editors will ask the agent about the writer's "platform," meaning the range of your media recognition, like Web sites, newspaper and magazine columns, and radio and TV appearances. You have to show how your book can be sold.

Editors and agents look for reasons to say no to a proposal. Give them the information and opportunity to say yes. You are the expert. Show your bona fides and be proud instead of shy. Use education, life experience, and clips to show how smart and cool you are.

The *competition* shows where your book will fit with others in the marketplace. Saying that there's no other book like yours gets people thinking there's a reason why. List three books in a similar area of interest, and damn with faint praise, always pointing out where yours is better. Agents want to see what other books exist so they understand how yours might be pitched. They also want evidence that your book is distinct and necessary.

Not like that. Like this. That's better.

Word-processing programs are there to save trees, not to confuse. The entire proposal should be in 12-point Times New Roman, double-spaced, with one-inch margins all around. One space after a period is enough and no hard returns at the end of every line. Switching typefaces and indiscriminate use of italic and bold-face make the pages look like you're demanding ransom for the return of the agent or editor's budgerigar, and they never got along with the bird anyhow.

I agree that sequentially numbered chapters are a patriarchal conceit, but they do have an appreciated simplicity.

Once all the pieces are assembled, put all the loose pages into a simple folder, no glow-in-the-dark color or cute stickers. The proposal needs to be straightforward. One publisher met with a New Orleans pastry chef and asked him to send a proposal for a cookbook. Instead of doing the admittedly tedious work, the chef sent a king cake to the offices on Shrove Tuesday, along with a nice card. The staff ate the cake. Another cake followed the next year and again the staff ate it. The chef stopped sending cakes. He's still waiting for a contract, and the staff has slimmed down.

Forget worrying about the writer photograph until you have a contract. Trust me.

The *inquiry letter* is easy after what you've been through writing the proposal. Though the letter goes out first and by itself, the proposal has to be ready in case an agent jumps at your hot idea. The focus of the letter is the *pitch*, a description of your book in twenty-five words or less. No agent will dig to find out what the damn thing is about. You have to tell them.

Even if Uncle Ted owns the company, go through an agent. An agent has a handle on what editors are looking for, the publisher's real abilities, and how to get you the best deal. Good agents will push your work from one selling season to the next, and occasionally pick up the tab for cocktails. This is important.

Do your homework and send inquiry letters only to agents who specialize in the subject area you're writing about. Romance-novel agents will respond to a self-help book inquiry with less than a raised eyebrow. Writer's conferences and workshops are great places to hear the gossip about who's a good agent looking for new writers, and whom to avoid. Sending an inquiry letter or proposal will cause separation anxiety. You've done well in reaching out. Wait a little longer.

FOR FICTION WRITERS

Of the 175,000 books published every year in this country ("How Many Books Are Too Many?" *The New York Times*, July 18, 2004), only 10,000 are fiction, and we are poorer for the imbalance. In a *Washington Post* interview, fatwa-dodging Salman Rushdie said, "The art of the novel, I think, is to open worlds to you, and it seems to me we live in a time when that's of desperate importance."

An MFA is no guarantee of the ability to write or of being published. Agents and editors want to be surprised with well-constructed and well-thought-out stories. Many novels by academics and writing-program alumni lack any juice. Some are quite competent structurally, except when you put down the book, you want to put it down the garbage chute. Where's the humanity? A strong writing course would stick students in a grungy single-resident-only hotel, give them Big Chief pads and lead pencils, and set them the assignment of getting down real stories, split infinitives and rude words included.

The *inquiry letter* jams the most intriguing elements of the story and characters on one page. This is no time to be verbose. Rewriting is essential.

Wait until you've completed the entire manuscript before sending inquiry letters to agents. Say you send out a letter before you're ready. They will respond, asking for the first fifty pages, and then, if it's as good as you believe, they'll demand the complete manuscript by FedEx. What are you going to do? To sell it, the agent needs the whole manuscript, not one almost done, pretty close, damn-near finished.

Include *work and life experience*, mention previously published short stories, anything to bolster the argument that your writing is hot. Leave out being on the high school newspaper.

Agents toss letters using "rollicking," "hilarious," "rib-tickling," or "surreal" to describe a novel unless a fifty-dollar bill is stapled to the top. They'll have a good lunch with the money and tell their assistant to throw the letter out.

Even fiction writers must *define the audience*, at least by gender and age. Everyone writes for an audience. If you're not writing for one, you're writing for yourself, so keep the work to journals and leave me out of it. We're not that close.

If your inquiry is turned down, this means the novel is not right for that agent. Publishing is entirely subjective and many times predicated on whether the agent or editor had a good night's sleep. Go to the next one on your list.

CONTRACT SHUFFLE
WITH AGENTS AND PUBLISHERS

FOR FICTION AND NONFICTION WRITERS

CONTRACTS KEEP LAWYERS gainfully employed. They're written for the sole benefit of publishers, and signed with the belief that the other party is untrustworthy and must be kept in line by threat of prosecution. The standard contract for agents and publishers is called a *boilerplate*, though some should be treated as made of papier-mâché instead of cast iron. Since every book and writer have different needs, never sign an un-negotiated boilerplate contract. The publisher is privileged to have the writer, and not the other way around. Be confident of your worth in the joint enterprise of getting a book to market. Always negotiate with the knowledge that the publisher needs your work.

The language of the contract is an indication of what to expect from the association. A mean contract demands everything for the agent or publisher and leaves little for the writer. Make sure you will receive fair earnings for your manuscript. This is not the time to be shy. Much can be negotiated, but the general tone of the contract remains. Run from the mean contract.

An agent offers you an *agency agreement*. Thrills abound in anticipation of fame. Sometimes. Signing with an agent is another part of the long, hard process. Before signing an agency agreement, do research on the agent to make sure he or she is the right one for you. Agents are public about their successes, and Internet searches show what books they have sold to whom. Visit www.publishersmarketplace.com and subscribe to *Publishers Lunch,* the online newsletter from nice folk who keep track of the deals.

Before signing a contract with an agent or publisher, join the

National Writers Union. Membership includes free contract advice from writers who know contracts from your perspective and are trained to review contracts clause by clause and teach members how to negotiate. The NWU also has advisers who specialize in author-agent contracts as well as author-publisher contracts. Publishing keeps changing, and the NWU is there with advocacy, grievance assistance, member education, and even a job hotline. See their Web site at www.nwu.org.

A good agent will be supportive, recommend a book midwife or editor if needed, suggest other projects, and keep open lines of communication. He or she will ride the in-house editor to give your book the attention it deserves. Send birthday and Christmas cards and pay attention to the agent's advice.

An agent's *memorandum of agreement* is a simple two-page contract for representation, and can be for one project or the writer's entire output with the *right of first refusal*. This right means the writer submits each project for the agent to consider for thirty days. If the agent takes a pass, the writer is entitled to take the work elsewhere.

Compensation is the meat of the memorandum. This is where you sign away 15 or 20 percent of the book's earnings, including foreign and theatrical rights. Think for a moment. Right now you have a stack of twenty-pound bond paper, worth five dollars if not printed with your opus. The agent can turn this liability into a cash stream, but be careful of the percentage points and don't give away your labor.

Publishers used to send royalty and other payments directly to agents, with them doing the dispensation. The agent held the payment for two weeks to process the paperwork, while the patient writer, living on credit cards, was hit with fines for late payment. The situation has improved and publishers now provide *split accounting*. The agent is sent a small check and the writer is sent a big check.

Either agent or writer can terminate the memorandum by letter. Unscrupulous agents have tried to seduce writers from their present agent with promises of riches and groupies. This never happens to the book midwife, who would sell members of his immediate family into slavery for a free lunch and dirty weekend with only one groupie.

Publishers are an odd bunch whose enthusiasm is tinged with melancholy.

Where the agency agreement is simple and friendly, the publishing contract is a tangle of legal language made to cover any possibility, including reprint rights on other planets and the reunification of Korea. Get this:

The rights granted to publisher, and publisher's licenses, under this agreement include the right to prepare, publish, use, adapt, reproduce, sell, and otherwise distribute electronic versions of the Work. The term "electronic versions" shall mean any and all methods of copying, recording, storage, retrieval, or delivery of all or any portion of the Work, alone or in combination with other works, including any multimedia work or electronic book; by any means now known or hereafter devised, including, without limitation, by electronic or electromagnetic means, or by analog or digital signal; whether in sequential or non-sequential order, in any and all physical media now known of or hereafter devised including, without limitation, magnetic tape, floppy disks, CD-ROM, DVD, game cartridges laser disk, optical disk, IC card or chip, eBook, sound recordings, programs for machine teachings, ephemeral screen flashings or reproductions thereof, Internet downloadable books, PDF, Adobe Reader, Microsoft Reader, Soft-Book, and any other human or machine-readable medium, whether or not permanently affixed in such media; and the broadcast and/or transmission thereof by any and all means now known or hereafter devised.

Scrimshaw rights anyone?

The former ten-page boilerplate contract has expanded in proportion to the increase in law school graduates each year. Time
is needed to go through each point to make sure the writer
receives what they need and the publisher is encouraged to work
for them.

A work is automatically under *copyright* once you put pen to
paper or finger to keyboard. The publisher *registers* the copyright,
not the writer. Let them pay the fees. Copyright registration provides the writer with further legal protection, and includes the
right to collect damages. The copyright should be registered in
the name of the writer, not the publishing company. Always.

Warranty and indemnity promises the publisher the work is original and free of scandal, obscenity, and libel, and if so, it's not their
fault. Any fees arising out of legal action against the work should
be split between publisher and writer. This is where an agent or
contract advisor earns their keep. If the writer turns snotty and
refuses to make requested changes to the work demanded by
legal action, the publisher can cancel the contract and request
return of any advance paid.

Next is *manuscript and delivery*. The complete manuscript must
arrive at a certain date in a certain condition. Whether you're an
old pro or first-time writer, hire an outside editor to make sure the
manuscript is in perfect shape. Permissions to reprint other sourc-
es have to be with the manuscript, along with tables, illustrative
material, and bibliography. The publisher has the right to edit the
work, except the editors are fighting with the marketing department in the conference room and both sides are losing.

You, the writer, are sent *galley proofs* or galleys of the manuscript,
formatted into a page design and set in type. This is your last opportunity to make any changes. If the changes are over 10 percent,
the publisher charges the writer's royalty account for the excess

amount, and the acquiring editor has to wash the coffee cups in the break room for a month as penance.

Advance and royalties appear late in the contract. An advance is against future royalties, not much more than a temporary loan. When talking to other writers, be vague about the dollar amount of your advance to raise maximum envy. *Publishers Lunch* provides a handy guide:

"nice deal" $1 to $49,000
"very nice deal" $50,000 to $99,000
"good deal" $100,000 to $250,000
"significant deal" $251,000 to $499,000
"major deal" $500,000 and up

Gross receipts or *net receipts* contract? Net happens when you can't get gross. Listen to your agent and the NWU contract advisers. Either contract can be sweetened by having the figure expand after a certain number of sales, known as an *escalator clause*, like fifteen percent for the first 50,000 copies sold, and twenty percent afterward.

Your book stinks—we want to publish it.

New Yorker CARTOON

Many writers get their knickers in a twist over *subsidiary rights*. To complete the book, the writer has put relationships at risk by ignoring them and worked at the keyboard until hit by sciatica. Along comes the publisher, demanding 50 percent from reprint or paperback sales, book-club editions, foreign-language rights, and second serial rights. *First serial rights*, like a chapter published in a magazine, are marginally fairer with 75 to 25 percent. The reason for the high split is contacts. Where the writer would bang on closed and locked doors, an editor at a publishing company makes a telephone call. The high split keeps the publisher interested and is worth their efforts.

Statements and payments are begun in January and July of each year, and sent out in March and September. The accounting department processes all the money accrued from sales and figures out how much goes to whom. Here is where the writer's royalty fits on a $20 book:

48% discount / $9.60 (Average between forty percent for independent booksellers to fifty-five percent for distributors and higher for book clubs and catalogs.)

18% overhead / $3.60 (Warehousing, collections, promotion, editorial, and returns.)

12% manufacturing costs / $2.40 (Paper, printing, and binding.)

10% writer's royalty / $2.00 (Gross receipts contract.)

6% sales representative's commission / $1.20

6% publisher's profit / $1.20

Book publishing is a $30-billion-a-year industry and growing. Where does the money go? Certainly not to your check. According to the September 26, 2005 issue of *New York Magazine,* the chairman and editor-in-chief of Alfred A. Knopf Publishing Group pulls in $750,000 a year. The president and publisher of Penguin Press gets a tidy $400,000. The CEO and vice-chairman of Barnes & Noble rakes in $4,813,567 a year, while the full time clerks at the stores make $12,896 for more hours and less fun. If you want to big money in books, forget writing. Take out a loan and buy Barnes & Noble.

The semiannual royalty check is diminished by *returns and overpayments.* What was hot one season chills in the following season. Seeing a book sell 4,000 copies in its first six months and twenty copies the next is not uncommon. The American book-buying public is a fickle tart, all giggles and promises while waiting for the newest bestseller. Books ordered by stores can be returned for credit, and they will be if not moving in the numbers the store needs to keep the lights on. A publishing company will keep back as much as 15 percent of the royalty check to cover the eventual returns. This is an unfortunate part of the cost of doing business.

Free copies and writer discount vary from company to company, and any writer wants more. Ten freebies is cheap, fifty is generous. If a writer gives workshops and lectures, he or she will want to do back-of-the-room sales and ask for a 40 percent discount with royalties paid, or 50 percent discount with no royalty. These sales can be triumphantly high or embarrassingly low.

"Let us make all the necessary vows that we will stick to the business of publishing the best books we can lay our hands on and then keep our hands on them for as long as may be." William Warder Norton wrote these fine sentiments in the 1920s when founding his company, W. W. Norton. There are *frontlist* books, the hoped-for bestsellers leading off the season; *midlist* books, the ones expected to sell but not spectacularly; and *backlist* books, dependable sellers whose annual march to the cash registers can be accurately predicted. All these books can die, especially nonfiction. *Discontinuance of publication* happens when the publisher has realized all the sales possible through their outlets, had the accounting department cut the book for not realizing enough profit, or lost interest. If the work falls out of print, the writer sends a request to have the rights reverted back to him or her. The publisher has sixty days to comply. In a friendly contract, the writer can buy the *means of manufacture*, disks or printing plates, for a cheap one-third of original cost, and find another publisher who might be able to find the missing audience.

The *option clause* is a nice bit of sleight-of-hand. Publishers want more than one book from a writer, and the option is the right of first refusal for the writer's next work. Ninety days are given for the decision. The negotiating of a contract gives the writer a case of the willies. They are run through the legal wringer and lose hope of getting anything from the publisher, when the acquiring editor leans over their desk and says, "I'll tell you what I'm going to do. No one can predict the future. We'll take out this clause so you can pursue any opportunities that come up." Of course the writer will take his or her next work to the devil they know, though the editor's magnanimity is appreciated.

The *cross-collateralization* or *cross-accounting* clause is evil and should be stricken from the contract, no room for disagreement. It means if you do several books for a publisher and one is unable to earn out its advance, they can charge the loss to the royalty account of your more successful book. Both parties take a gamble with every book, the writer with their time and wits, and the publisher with money. If each can win, each can lose graciously as well. Ever try to get a refund at the racetrack when your horse stumbles out of the gate and comes in seventh?

Uncle Ted owns the company and has promised several thousand dollars in marketing and publicity money. There is no reason to trust him, especially when you consider how he has treated Aunt Hilda. Get any extras written in *riders* in the contract. This includes design approval, marketing budgets, and anything not covered in the pages. Handshakes and promises over lunchtime glasses of Chardonnay are quickly forgotten.

Have a preemptive bout of seller's remorse before signing the contract. Is the company you're throwing in with the right one for your book, do they have the right proportion of integrity to practicality, will they be responsive to your book? You can still walk away. A twinge of worry will wait and turn into blind panic later.

If you're in, the book midwife is with you, sticking until the end, galley proofs included.

FRESH HOPE FOR A FIRST DRAFT

DO YOU REALLY want to write the book? Many want to have written a book instead of sitting down and sweating over the keyboard. Do you have any idea what this means? Let me tell you.

FOR FICTION AND NONFICTION WRITERS

All writing is a campaign against cliché. Not just clichés of the pen but clichés of the mind and clichés of the heart.

MARTIN AMIS

Working to a schedule now will help when the deadlines begin. Figure out how long it takes you to complete a chapter and make the date. Collaborating with a book midwife means you must have the material in their hands on time. Many are nocturnal creatures and will call at two in the morning from loneliness or for muffin recipes if they don't have a manuscript to edit.

Get to your desk by 6:00 AM and start before you're awake. The first draft is about generating material in a cohesive form. The cut, slice, and dice happen later when your confidence kicks in.

"I can write." Since you know how to drive, you can build a car, right? Other than reference books on your subject, the most helpful to have piled on the left side of your desk are books on grammar and usage. Word-processing software comes with spelling and grammar checking, and they suck without your engagement. The English language deserves to be treated with a certain respect. Know your predicates, prepositions, subordinate clauses, and restrictive and nonrestrictive phrases, and all the rest of the fun.

Publishing nomenclature has writer and author as interchangeable or divided between the writer as unpublished and the author published. Hogwash to both. A writer does the work, and an author has done the work. A writer continues to push his books and has as his final words, "I guess we'll have to cancel next week's reading in Portland." An author is already dead and enshrined in a Modern Library edition, like Joseph Heller, or so debilitated that his or her last words are, "Get me a toothpick."

(Always do your homework before writing a screed. In this instance, author is from the Old French, *auctor,* and the Latin, *auctorem*. The word appeared in the English language in the late fourteenth century and means "enlarger, founder, and one who writes statements." None of these definitions approaches the actual work. The writer's main purpose is to tell stories.)

Writers write every day, even when they aren't writing. Always take a notebook and pen when leaving the house for a walk or run. Eavesdrop on conversations, describe a storefront, and look at how people are dressed. What seems useless today will be helpful tomorrow.

California writers go to therapists. New York writers gobble down antidepressants. Writers in the rest of the country get by on beer. Changing therapists or switching beers in the middle of a project is fine. Going for a new medication is asking for drug-induced mood swings. This will upset your book midwife.

Everyone has a personal style of working, from neat stacks of research material to an explosion of papers tossed around the workspace. Some have music blaring, and others depend on silence. Find your style and stick to it, though the style changes depending on the project. No one is watching, and the teacher will not ask to see how you solved a certain problem. Results are the most important.

When in doubt, use "that" in place of "which." "Which" needs a preceding comma and a brougham.

Writing makes us weepy and fragile creatures. Any criticism possible to be construed as negative will be. Hide your manuscript from spouses, girlfriends, boyfriends, and regular friends until you're ready.

Do you smoke? At age sixty-seven, novelist Colleen McCullough lost the sight in one eye to macular degeneration, made worse by her tobacco habit. She's still writing and smoking. "The words are in the cigarettes," she said. (I do not encourage debilitating vices such as smoking, unless fine French tobaccos are involved and the writer is kind enough to share.)

Write straightforward, no-junk-in-the-trunk, declarative sentences. Here is a good sentence: "The dog walked down the street."

Writing is telling a story, and this goes for nonfiction, too. If the writing obscures the story, the reader is lost and the book is tossed. Style is the words you choose and how you see events. Creative writing teachers who harp about style and voice over content should be given unassisted tours of the Marianas Trench. As you write with greater clarity, your individual style will emerge.

Keep punctuation to commas and periods. The em dash is supposed to signal an abrupt change in thought. Why not start a new sentence or paragraph? Only Herman Melville is allowed to use the semicolon in fiction. He's dead, by the way.

Of the many dumb saws about writing, "Write what you know" ranks high. Write what you read. Have everything published by Richard Feynman? You're a science geek. Nuts about Patricia Highsmith? Go for the mystery. Writers writing what they know leads to long, dull books about personal hygiene, and no one can make flossing interesting.

More and more, over and over, again and again, and faster and faster are impossibilities. Faster is already faster, and more is already more. Stop this nonsense.

Use your outline from the proposal to stay on track. Let the chapters change where they must, but following a tight outline will keep nonessential tangents to a minimum. One writer who will not be named (sorry, Brian) works with a graphic artist to develop a cover for the book, and uses this as his only reference throughout writing. He's done a dozen books with his scary procedure, none suitable for mixed company.

Forget about being original. You already are. No one has sensed what you have, traveled to the places you've been, or lived where you've lived. Be fresh instead of worrying after the elusive and intangible new. Take your prose into the shower and scrub off the arch phrases and literary flourishes. Be sure to get behind the ears and rinse out the gooey stuff between the toes.

The classic Greek argument is thesis, antithesis, synthesis, not prosthesis, hypothesis, narcissus. Where did you go to school?

Research means going to the library and hitting the stacks. Anything gleaned from the Internet should be checked and rechecked for accuracy. A poem beginning, "Come to the edge / We might fall / Come to the edge / It's too high!" is attributed across the Internet as being written by Guillaume Apollinaire. Even Margaret Thatcher has quoted the piece. Digging beyond the resources of Google shows Christopher Logue as the real source of the poem. He wrote the piece for a poster announcing an Apollinaire exhibition in London in the early 1960s.

That's okay. Many have made the same mistake, though a touch more elegantly.

A friend calls and asks what you are doing.
WRITER: Writing. I have three chapters to finish this week.
FRIEND: That's easy. Let's go to a movie.
If writing is so easy, why isn't the friend at home knocking out pages? The only people who understand what you're doing are other writers. Seek out writers' conferences and workshops for solace, and online communities such as *www.readerville.com*. Make sure the twit who thinks writing is a breeze has to pay retail when your book hits the stands.

Composition is the proper word in the proper place. If you think either is easy, you're not working hard enough.

This is your book and you get the final word, except for passive sentence construction and other things the book midwife will think of later.

Vocabulary ain't all it's cracked up to be. What's important is the use of the words. Story dictates all. A mush-mouth of big words gets in the way.

Join a writers' group with caution. They can devolve into bitching about politics and general gossip, and waste time you could put to better use by writing. Fiction writers belong in fiction writers' groups, and nonfiction writers belong in nonfiction writers' groups. There's little to be gained for either party in the wrong group. If you find a solid, supportive group of people who are serious about their work and give intelligent criticism, hold tight to them.

"Dystopia," as defined by Webster's, is "an imaginary place where people lead dehumanized and often fearful lives." "Meniscus" is "the curved upper surface of a column of liquid." Use either word in any context and I'll see to it you're forced to watch network television. *Desperate Housewives* is supposed to be pretty cool, and available on DVD if the show is canceled.

That's too bad. Get back to work.

Making the commitment to write a book does not give you license to be a schmuck. The artistic temperament is pure nonsense. Writing demands as much dedication and knowledge as being an orthopedic surgeon, and the surgeon is neither allowed to be surly nor praised for a lack of basic social skills. Writing comes from the desire to understand humanity and the life around you. Do the laundry, play with the kids, take your partner out for dinner, and be decent to people while doing your work. This will inform your writing, not diminish it.

FOR FICTION WRITERS

Manners are of such great consequence to the novelist that any kind will do. Bad manners are better than no manners at all, and because we are losing our customary manners, we are probably overly conscious of them; this seems to be a condition that produces writers.

FLANNERY O'CONNOR

What the story is about, who is involved, and where it happens begins in the first paragraph of the first page.

Point of view is defined by the story. Listen to the story to find what point of view is appropriate. The story knows.

FIRST PERSON: *I watched the dog walk down the street.*

If the "I" dominates the narrative, there's no room left for the reader. The "I" has to be inclusive.

SECOND PERSON: *You watch the dog walk down the street.*

Direct address is exhausting for the length of a novel, and best used in combination with first or third person.

THIRD PERSON: *The dog walked down the street.*

Be cautious of detachment. Let the reader in on why the dog and the street are important.

THIRD PERSON OMNISCIENT: *The dog walked down the street while thinking of his water bowl.*

The narrative voice sees all, even into the hiding places. This can cause a story to stall instead of flow.

Story is character, action, setting, and atmosphere. A character lives the action in the story, and is not lived by the action. Setting is the apartment, hotel, living room, and corner bar. Atmosphere is sunny and bright or dark and malicious. Tension holds the whole package together.

Calm your worries. This will be rewritten a minimum four times before seeing a press.

The heart will sustain you more than technical virtuosity. Novelist James Lee Burke, Pulitzer Prize nominee and winner of two Edgar Allan Poe awards, started writing fiction in college. His English prof returned one of his stories with a "D" and the remarks, "Your spelling is an assault upon the eyeballs. Your penmanship makes me wish the Phoenicians had not developed the alphabet. But I couldn't give you an F because you have so much heart."

Character is an epic story. See Homer's *The Odyssey.*

"I can write." What about telling a story with a beginning, middle, and end, characters who breathe, and rooms so real you bump into the furniture?

There are the nasty words, the "F" word and the "S" word and the others in between. A New York editor told one writer, "We're looking to break you out to a wide audience. No 'F' word until page fifty. By that time they are stuck in the story and if the word upsets them, it's too late." The same editor also limited the writer to twenty "F" words per novel.

Use complete names, first and last, when introducing a character, unless there's a solid reason against this. Spell the character's name the same throughout the entire manuscript. So far, you have Rodriguez as Rodrigues, Rodriquez, Rodriques, and Roderigués.

A story is made of characters, and each needs a distinctive attribute to make him or her real for the reader. Compare your characters to the list below and see where they succeed or fail.

PASSIVE: Things happen to them outside of their control, and the most they do is blame their mothers, who are probably at fault anyway. Passive characters make for a victim novel, anathema to readers.

PRESENT: They are there the same as a fire hydrant or STOP sign, helpful only on occasion.

ACTIVE: Here is the meat. They propel the story forward and give it definition. An active character can be proactive or reactive.

AGGRESSIVE: This kind of character, like the real people he or she mirrors, is a pain in the ass. Reserve for villains and make sure something terrible happens to them.

Descriptions of color, texture, and scent define a place and person, and give the story more depth. Use your senses.

Conflict derives from the characters having different goals and is essential to driving the story.

Call if you get too serious. Hundreds of bad limericks are ready for recitation.

Dialog is a monster for everyone. People communicate with gesture and intonation as much as words. Record and transcribe any conversation with a friend:

WRITER: "He's so, you know."
FRIEND: "Yeah, I know. Like always."
WRITER: "That thing he did."
FRIEND: "Jeez. That's not the only time."

Are you talking about politics, sex, religion, or pet care? This is also painful for the reader, who regrets paying $14.95 plus tax for the book. Dialog must be immediate and full of information.

The use of tags in dialog, also known as identifiers and attributives, is another scaly beast. In the 1930s and 1940s, Lester Dent wrote the pulp novels featuring Doc Savage, Man of Bronze. Dent's *The Fantastic Island* represents the worst in tag usage. One of Doc's five pals, Monk, growls belligerently, grunts, demands, bellows, and squalls through the first chapter. Using only "he said," and "she said" means the dialog alone has to carry the freight. Verbs and adverbs should be used sparingly. Do the work.

Movies are movies and books are books. Kurt Vonnegut wrote: "The worst thing about film, from my point of view, is that it cripples illusions which I have encouraged people to create in their heads. Film doesn't create illusions. It makes them impossible. It is a bullying form of reality, like the model rooms in the furniture department of Bloomingdale's.

"There is nothing for the viewer to do but gawk. For example: there can be only one *Clockwork Orange* by Stanley Kubrick. There are tens of thousands of *Clockwork Orange* by Anthony Burgess, since every reader has to cast, costume, direct, and design the show in his head." Vonnegut is being overly cranky, but the basic admonition is to realize the difference between mediums and write the novel as a novel.

Conversation overheard in coffee shop: "I know that pure stream of consciousness is what I write right now." Please don't. Please.

Frustration is a large part of writing. To get a character in and out of a room with something interesting to say is hard. There's no formula to fall back on. You're on your own. Accept the gift of frustration and use the energy to keep going.

Doubting means you think you can do better. Give it a shot, but be wary of overwriting. Keep the language clear and direct. Writing is the mistress of story. Give the story what it wants.

Your first, middle, and last loyalties are to your story and characters. Except for the book midwife, everyone else can go spin. This includes well-meaning advice from family members, husbands, wives, girlfriends, and boyfriends. How many books have they written?

Holding your work up to another novel will drive you nuts. One day a reader will get hold of your finished book and loudly lament, "I'll never be able to write as well as (your name here)!" Read comic books and soup-can labels. The only novel to compare yours with is yours.

Drink plenty of water.

Charles Lutwidge Dodgson, who cranked out a couple of fanciful tales under the pen name Lewis Carroll, complained to a friend, "I'm beginning to think that the proper definition of 'Man' is 'an animal that writes letters.'"

  Close, but no reason to light a Cohiba. The proper definition of humans may be "an animal who tells stories."

Add fact to fiction and keep the story in the real world. The real world is weirder than anything you could dream up.

Humor is a way of seeing the world and cannot be forced. Henry Miller said, "To the person who thinks with his head, life is a comedy. To those who think with their feelings, or work through their feelings, life is a tragedy." Drama does not exclude humor, but uses it to give definition and temporary respite from a somber tone.

Only Dorothy Parker is allowed to use alcohol while writing. She's dead, by the way.

Delete the word "totally" from your vocabulary. Throw out "awesome" as well.

Historical fiction is written for readers who enjoy the genre and also know their history very well. Much research is needed if going this route. The readership will catch you on any shortcuts and give you a deserved pummeling.

Book midwives are professionals. This makes us right. Accept it.

Writing fiction demands a form of self-hypnosis to get into the heads of the characters, and this gives the story a welcome authenticity.

If your current pages lack the emotional power of previous chapters, remember, this is a first draft. Sometimes the writing is uneven, which is why writing is rewriting. The scenes are important and the rest is application.

Everything's going to be fine. Drink more water.

Pay attention. The inverted participle phrase does not make good writing. "The dog walked down the street," not "Down the street, the dog walked."

Only Ken Kesey is allowed to use recreational drugs while writing. He's dead, by the way.

The jitteriness, pacing the floor, and general lack of confidence is normal. Who are you to think you have something interesting to say? The days and nights at the keyboard should have been spent looking for a real job.

Take heart. The book midwife says you are writing interesting things and more will come. Let doubt open you to being a better writer. Wipe your sniffles and flex your fingers. You have a book to write.

The ending separates the writers from the dilettantes. When you're down to the last hundred pages, you're closing in on the end, and this starts sooner than most people think. The end sells the story to the reader, more so than the beginning or middle. If it's satisfying (meaning an outgrowth of the characters and plot arcs), readers will have the story banging around inside their skull plates for years and enjoy the noise.

If you're too tired to write, drink coffee. If that's not enough, smoke cigarettes.

A HEALTHY WRITER
IS A WRITING WRITER

SITTING IN FRONT of a computer screen for long periods of time will cause back problems and eyestrain, and make you grouchy when you should be enjoying your work. You can ease most attacks of sciatica with hot Epsom salt baths, but your back and eyes need preventative attention. See your doctor for any health problems. Your book midwife will want a note.

While these exercises will make the sessions more comfortable, nothing beats aerobic exercise to jack up your heart rate and knock the dust off the overstuffed shelves of your brain. Walk, swim, bicycle, or join a gym to sweat among sweaty people three to five times a week. Make healthy meals part of your work schedule, with fresh fruit and vegetables and whole grains. Prepackaged processed junk foods make for lousy manuscripts. Drink plenty of water, take vitamin supplements and gingko biloba, and be the envy of those out-of-shape couch slugs who only dream about writing a book.

Dressing comfortably does not mean a sweatshirt and sweatpants with Ben & Jerry stains. The book midwife puts finger to keyboard wearing a formal, wing-collar white shirt, gray over-the-calf cotton socks, and red-and-blue-striped boxer shorts, pants optional. Nothing less will do.

The Authors Guild has group health and dental plans for published book writers in New York State, Massachusetts, California, Connecticut, New Jersey, southern Florida, and Chicago. Dues in the organization run $90 for the first year and follow a sliding scale based on writing income. Contact the guild at www.authorsguild .org or e-mail staff@authorsguild.org.

FOR THE EYES

With your fingertips, tap your chin and move up the face, tapping cheeks and under the eyes and your eyebrows. Press the eyebrows from where they start to the arch of the brow. Tap your temples to the back of your head and behind your earlobes. Feels good, right? Rub the base of your skull and under your earlobes, and rub your neck. Tap along the neck.

Rub your left shoulder and chest and along the underside of your left arm. Put your thumb in the pit of your left elbow and let it sway. Rub along your left arm to your wrist and take care of the fingers. Squeeze your left hand. Repeat for the right side, no cheating or shortcuts.

Repeat the whole process ten times.

While waiting for your computer to boot up or coffee to brew, wiggle your eyebrows ten times. Compose saucy dialog full of double-entendres.

Let your head drop as you exhale. Inhale while lifting your head and blinking your eyes. Purse your lips and blow out stale air while turning your head clockwise two and a half times until you end where you began. Think of T. S. Eliot's "Little Gidding" from *Four Quartets*, not "The Love Song of J. Alfred Prufrock." Do the exercise again, turning counterclockwise. Do each turn five times, and complete the exercise ten times.

Hold the finger you use to punish your mouse three inches in front of your face. Turn your head side to side and keep your eyes on the finger. Repeat ten times with your eyes wide open and another ten with your eyes shut. Count out each complete set and take in a big breath when your eyes are shut, and let out a big breath when your eyes open. Do this one hundred times.

While the printer is churning out pages of double-spaced 12-point Times New Roman, lay your palms over your eyes and visualize ecstatic reviews in your publication of choice. Doing this three times a day will not be deducted from your time in paradise.

Stand up from your chair and plant your feet eight or nine inches apart. Turn side to side and keep your torso and head in one line, and let your relaxed arms do the swinging. Keep your eyes looking forward and do ten complete turns with your eyes wide open and ten more with your eyes shut. Do this one hundred times.

FOR THE BACK

Pain, agony, and torture will not make better writing. Comfort will. Make sure you have a decent chair with proper lumbar support, or at least add a cushion to do the job.

Do sit-ups before going to your desk. Lie down on the floor and raise your shoulders as you keep your chin tucked in. Touch your knees with your fingers and count to five. Keep your back straight. Do five times in the morning and afternoon, and work up to ten times.

Next are leg lifts. Lie on your right side and bend your right leg a bit. Stretch your right arm flat and use this for balance as you line up your shoulder and hips. Lift your left leg about ten inches and lower the leg slowly. Do this five times, and do the same for your left side and your right leg. Do five times in the morning and afternoon, and work up to ten times.

To take care of your neck, sit in your chair. Press against your forehead with your hand and use your neck muscles to push against your hand. Press against your temple with your hand and use your neck muscles to push against your hand. Yes, the temple and forehead are two different areas. Count to ten and do six more times on each side. Put your hands behind your head and use your neck muscles to press against your hands. Count to ten and do six more times.

Do this to stretch your lower back. Lie on your back and raise your left knee to your chest. Hold on to your knee with your hands and count to three. Relax and repeat with your right leg. Do this ten times each side.

A good habit to develop is standing every half hour and stretching. Bend your knees enough to rattle the crease in your trousers, put your hands on the back of your shapely waist, and stretch to look at the ceiling. The acoustic tiles need replacing. Count to five and slowly straighten up. Do this five times.

The hamstring takes a beating when you sit for too long. This muscle runs from the hip down the back of the thigh all the way to the knee, and is in charge of back and hip flexibility. Stretch this muscle like you care. Your hamstring cares about you.

To stretch while standing, stand with your left leg straight out in front and rest your foot on your chair. Bend your right leg until you feel a slight stretch under your left thigh. Count to three and do the other leg. Do this five times.

To stretch while sitting, sit on the floor with your left leg straight out in front of you and your right leg bent with your foot flat on the floor. Lean toward your right leg until you feel a slight stretch under your left thigh. Count to three and do the other leg. Do this five times.

To stretch lying down, lie on your back with your knees bent and your feet flat on the floor. Raise your left leg slowly and place your hands behind your knee for support. Straighten your leg until you feel a slight stretch along the back of your thigh. Count to three and do the other leg. Do this five times.

Tension is part of the job and so is releasing the tension. Stand and roll your shoulders forward ten times. Roll backward ten times. Do the complete exercise ten times, as often during the day as you need.

HOW TO WORK WITH
AN IN-HOUSE EDITOR

EVERY PUBLISHING COMPANY, regardless of size, has a hierarchy. The independent publishers act like the big outfits, and the big outfits act big. *Executive management* is the owner, chief operating officer, executive vice president, and vice president of finance and accounting. *Sales and marketing staff* includes the vice president of marketing, marketing director, marketing manager and their associates and assistants, vice president of sales, national accounts director, sales manager, publicity director and their associates and assistants, and rights director and associate. *Production* has the production director, art director, interior and cover designers, and production associates and assistants.

The *editorial director* or *editor-in-chief* frets over editorial strategy and day-to-day operations, approves advances and contracts, and runs the profit and loss statements for each book. The *senior editor* acquires new books, negotiates contracts and advances, and rides production to make sure the books come out on time. A *developmental editor* does the editing of a manuscript, checks permissions, and communicates with the writer about any changes.

A plain, unadorned *editor* does the same as the senior editor, with the added responsibility of budgets and attending editorial meetings, and representing the writer's book when needed to other departments. *Associate editors* do whatever the editor tells them to do. *Editorial assistants* do whatever the entire editorial team tells them to do. *Proofreaders* read for accuracy, punctuation, and spelling, and *copyeditors* correct inconsistencies and ensure that all the corrections make sense.

Your point person inside the publishing company will be the editor. He or she is overworked and never paid enough, and besides your manuscript, has twenty or fifty others in need of attention.

Editors are stuck in meetings all day and work weekends on manuscripts to stay behind instead of overwhelmed. They can be distant, snotty, and impatient on occasion from work-related stress. This is not a reflection on you.

Even though you've worked with a book midwife, your manuscript is returned with questions, queries, and changes. Editors know their house styles and audiences. Pay attention.

Your editor is a professional skeptic, not a cynic. They ask questions to be convinced of your argument or story. Be satisfied when they are. A cynic is only a romantic who dresses badly.

Editorial costs are constantly under assault within companies. Publishers prefer spending money where they can see results, like billboards and magazine ads. A young woman with a New York company had walked the career hallway from editorial assistant and associate editor, and just acquired her first book by an established writer. The final manuscript arrived and she opened the package and began marking the pages with her blue pencil. Her supervisor peeked around the corner of her cubicle and asked what she was doing. "Editing the manuscript." "Stop," she was told. "Send it to production and get to the marketing meeting. That's what you're supposed to be doing." The woman went to the meeting, but ignored her supervisor and took the manuscript home. She pulled all-nighters to keep the book on schedule. When the writer saw what the editor had done, he sent roses.

The competition for your book is not outside the company, but inside with the other books to be published the same season. This another reason to be kind to your editor. They talk up the book with the sales staff.

Arguing with an editor's assessment is like paper training a weasel. Why bother? The assessment is subjective and based on stacks of reading and loads of experience. The editor's job is to make your book the best possible.

Before contacting the editor, direct any questions to your agent, who might have the answers.

Be nice to your editor. Never send a note like Henry James did after being asked to cut three lines from a 5,000-word article for the *Times Literary Supplement*: "I have performed the necessary butchery. Here is the bleeding corpse."

The relationship with an editor is based on business, not personality. You have entered into a contract to provide a product. The editor is not your pal, father confessor, confidante, faith healer, or matchmaker. Friendships do develop in working relationships, but to expect them is foolish. Keep it straight.

Contact your editor by e-mail. The telephone invites frustration by the careening pinball of voice mail. Short questions receive quick answers.

The question every editor wants to hear is, "How can I help you?" Ask this sincerely and do what you can with the answer.

Keep a paper trail of all communication with your editor. When returning a manuscript, include a letter of transmittal with any outstanding questions. After a telephone conversation, send an e-mail outlining what decisions and promises were made.

When you work well with an editor, follow him or her as they move from company to company for higher wages, greater flexibility in what they can acquire, and corner offices on higher floors. One writer is so loyal to his editor that he has followed him from Henry Holt to Little Brown, to Hyperion, to Doubleday, to Simon & Schuster. Next stop Random House?

Editors want recognition for their hard work. A mention in your acknowledgments is nice, as is a tin of homemade pralines.

If you're having a complete, irrational meltdown of worry over your book, call your book midwife, who charges by the hour and is used to the screaming. Your editor might not be so patient.

REWRITING AND THE
WORD-WATCH LIST

FOR FICTION AND NONFICTION WRITERS

THE MANUSCRIPT IS COMPLETE, you say, done and done with, and ready to roll. Nope, but this is time to take a breather from the work. Print out three copies and send them to readers who agree to return the manuscript in one week. Ask specific questions about content, plot, characters, and readability, and have them write comments in the margins and on the backs of pages. Two of the readers are people you know are able to read critically and be unselfish with praise and sneers. The third reader is your Aunt Hilda. She's always said you were talented, even in the play in third grade where you played a shrub. "Such emotional greenery," she said. "I wept when you were trimmed by the gardener."

Take long walks, shoot hoops, watch black-and-white Italian movies, and forget your manuscript until the copies are returned. Collate the pages so you have three page ones, three page twos, and so on, and put this stack to the left of your keyboard. If the criticism cuts too deep, turn to Aunt Hilda's congratulatory note. "Such emotional writing," she wrote. "I wept when the pages ran out." Type the comments in boldface where they belong on the electronic copy, and then recycle the paper manuscripts. Start rewriting at the beginning, line by line, and page by page.

Checking your research and adding new material takes less time than complaining about having to do it.

In *If You Want to Write,* Brenda Ueland said, "Now some people when they sit down to write and nothing special comes, no good ideas, are so frightened that they drink a lot of strong coffee to hurry them up, or smoke packages of cigarettes, or take drugs or get drunk. They do not know that good ideas come slowly, and that the more clear, tranquil and unstimulated you are, the slower the ideas come but the better they are." What does she know? Rewrites take more cigarettes and coffee than the first draft, or, if you want to follow Ueland's advice, more green tea and sugarless gum.

Be mean, vicious, and cruel to anything resembling a cliché. Thinking outside the box and dropping into a downward spiral are forbidden. These crutches make for dull reading and few readers.

Stay away from the dreaded slang unless your story needs it to establish time. This means no shock and awe, getting or coming down, tripping, throwing a spaz, digging it, groove, so not into or so into anything, and no hip whatever. These age a story faster than shelf dust.

Rewriting is where the story begins jumping on the page. Your favorite writers are not demigods whose words flow from them in perfect order. They have to crank through multiple drafts.

The screen gives you nothing, and staring out the window at the starlings is boring. You want to make the chapter work but something is missing. Take a pen and notebook to your neighborhood coffee shop and start writing longhand. Leave off flirting with the cute barista. That's better. Go home and get back to work.

"Paradigm" is out, finished, banned, inapplicable, and a dumb word repeated by people with no idea what the damn thing means. The same goes for "paradigmatic."

The WORD-WATCH LIST will help you hunt down the repetition of nouns, adjectives, and adverbs, especially in consecutive sentences. This happens to every writer, and is best not to worry about until rewriting. The worst are generalizations like some, almost, about, and any. Your name on the cover means you know everything about the subject or story. The reader appreciates specifics.

Have a notepad by your keyboard and write down the repeated words you find while reading your manuscript. What follows are some of the most common offenders. Once you complete your list, use the search function of your word-processing program to find the words and replace appropriately. No fair trying to do a blanket search and replace.

about
all
almost
any / anything
back
begin / began
better
break
broke / broken
bust / busted
but
calm / calmer / calmest
care / caring
complain / complained / complaining
complaint
consider / considered / considering
cry / cried / crying
dominant
every
exhaust / exhausted / exhausting
exist / existed / existing
excite / exciting
feel / feeling
glad-hand / glad-handed / glad-handing

good
happy / happiness
home
house
key
kind / kindness
know / knowing
knowledge
life
line / lined / lining
live / lived / living
my
never
new / newest / newer
now
old style
old-fashion / old-fashioned
or
own
pace / paced / pacing
passion / passionate
plan / planned / planning
pleasure
practice / practiced / practicing
promise / promised / promising
quick / quickly / quickest
scream / screamed / screaming
some / something
sudden / suddenly
then
time
too
tough / tougher / toughest

up
without
whimper / whimpered / whimpering
whine / whined / whining
work / worked / working

Unless you're a graduate of the British public school system, there's no "upwards" or "towards," only "upward" and "toward." The difference between British and American English is that we're right and they still spell color and favor with the archaic "u."

"Gentleman" and "gentlemen," and "lady" and "ladies" are stilted and mannered. Dump them. "Man" and "men," and "woman" and "women" do fine.

FOR FICTION WRITERS

You've done what others have only talked about, written a novel from beginning to end. Characters, action, setting, and atmosphere form a coherent story. Rewriting makes the story live for the reader.

The ellipsis shows where a sentence or word is missing from a quote. Using the three dots in fiction leads to fascist sympathies and sexual obsession with young ballerinas, like Louis-Ferdinand Céline. He's dead, by the way.

There is magic in rewriting. Characters speak their own language and rooms fill with furniture.

"I can't write," says the beginning writer. "Why did I think I could?" Stop thinking about writing and be a storyteller. The writing will take care of itself.

Punctuation creates mood. In his novel, *One Step Behind,* Henning Mankell imbues a scene with ominous tension by terse sentences and little punctuation except for periods and the occasional comma: "A private road lined with big trees led up to a two-storey house. A BMW was parked in front. Wallander got out of his car and rang the bell. No one answered. He banged on the door and rang again. It was 2 PM. He was sweating."

Outlines are a drag and you have to do one. Be an adult and quit complaining. List each chapter and what happens with characters, plot, and subplots. Having the entire story in your head is impossible, regardless of length. Read the outline carefully, and follow the logic of each character's actions and position in the story.

Leave "bombazine" to the third-rate Dickensians with their dippy nostalgia for an idealized nineteenth century. There has to be another name for twill-woven silk dyed black. Ditch "flaybottomist" and "jobbernole" as well. Write the present-day story in present-day vernacular.

"The dog walked down the street" has all you'd want from a sentence, but needs a bit more to give color and show its importance in the story.

Specify the dog so it enters the story, a mutt or a golden retriever.

How it walks gives an emotional quality, a stagger, a skip, or hip dysplasia.

The street shows atmosphere, a suburban neighborhood or derelict downtown.

Rewrite the sentence as: *The spindly, dun-colored mutt staggered along the broken sidewalk.*

With the addition of "He watched," the dog becomes a symbol of the observer's despair. The scene takes on weight. Fun stuff, right?

Much of rewriting concerns what's hidden in the basement. Character is defined by what's underneath as well as the ruling passion. Who is the character?

Physical descriptions are not ruggedly handsome, beautiful, and good-looking. Rip out any of these you find. Unless you're writing a police procedural, there's no reason to detail all the features of a face. Concentrating on one or two aspects give the reader's imagination room to fill in the rest. Take your notebook back to the neighborhood coffee shop and look at people. If the cute barista is still there, trade telephone numbers.

FINAL MANUSCRIPT

FOR FICTION AND NONFICTION WRITERS

The last thing we discover in writing a book is what to put first.

BLAISE PASCAL

YOU'VE WRITTEN YOUR BOOK from notes jotted on matchbook covers, three-by-five file cards, and journals, to hours at your PC invoking retinal burn. The rewrites should have been easier instead of hard, and somewhere took a left turn and became enjoyable for their own sake. This is a final primping before going to the party.

Novelist Jim Harrison recommends starting the writing day with a bowl of oatmeal to keep the cholesterol down, and dancing. Many writers work in too enclosed a space for serious high stepping, and besides, a white male heterosexual lumbering through a rumba is plain horrifying to imagine.

Singing is the better alternative, especially helpful when becoming too tense. Whistle or hum, and your choice of volume will keep the song as public or private as you want. Use this list as a beginning. Loading your iPod with the songs is unacceptable. Vocalizing calls down the muses to help untangle plot points and grammatical problems, correct spelling, and keep you honest.

If I Only Had a Brain
(Ray Bolger / E.H. Harburg and Harold Arlen)
Belt out with brio to keep humility humming along.

Gotta Get Up
(Harry Nilsson / Harry Edward Nilsson)
You used to be fun. Now you work. Celebrate the change.

Ain't that Peculiar?
(Marvin Gaye / William "Smokey" Robinson, Marvin Tarplin, Robert Rogers, and Warren Moore)
The sun is shining and you sit inside hunched over a keyboard. What would you call it?

Nowhere to Run
(Martha and the Vandellas / Brian Holland, Lamont Dozier, and Eddie Holland)
The best solution to a sentence ending in a preposition is adding the word "baby."

Bile Chant
(The Wonder Stuff / Miles Hunt)
For emergencies only, like when overpowered by visions of fluffy bunnies and other nice thoughts.

Boobs A Lot
(The Fugs / Steve Weber)
Sour and dour? Let this loosen your muscles.

Why Can't I Be Good?
(Lou Reed / Lou Reed)
Best rendered while wearing dark, dark sunglasses and black leather trousers, and in a dark, dark mood.

Innocent When You Dream
(Tom Waits / Tom Waits and Kathleen Brennan)
No explanation necessary. We are innocent when we dream.

Twisted
(Lambert, Hendricks and Ross / Annie Ross and Wardell Grey)
A reminder to make your words bounce, jump, and jive, and get prescriptions refilled.

The Vatican Rag
(Tom Lehrer / Tom Lehrer)
Nothing is sacred, everything is permitted on the printed page.

Boulevard of Broken Dreams
(Marianne Faithfull / Al Dubin and Harry Warren)
Gigolo and gigolette enjoy the editing process with a laugh today
and cry tomorrow.

Tears of a Clown
(Smokey Robinson and the Miracles / William "Smokey" Robinson, Stevie Wonder, and Hank Cosby)
Break out your unused falsetto to jump-start stalled brain cells.

Sometimes your only recourse is to "cowboy the fuck up." The
phrase comes from Boston Red Sox first baseman Kevin Millar.
During the 2003 season, he rallied the Sox with "Cowboy up" and
Sox fans filled baseball chat rooms with the ruder version. The Red
Sox won the World Series in 2004, proving this works. "Cowboy
the fuck up" means, yeah, go ahead and whimper, then get back
to work, be tough, and do the job regardless of how hopeless it
seems. Writing is not for the weak of head or heart, and a more
butch endeavor ain't been revealed.

Use in the following situations:

Behind schedule? CTFU.

Eyes are bloodshot? CTFU.

Computer screen is frozen? Write in your notebook and
CTFU.

Butt hurts from sitting? Walk around the block and CTFU.

When in doubt, CTFU.

You've lost your tone. Not your muscle tone, but how you say what
you want to say. The thing is more important than how the thing
is said. Focus on the idea and the tone will correct itself.

Damn, you're writing. Your latest chapter is very cool, direct, and immediate, and the published book will be a bargain at full retail price.

Books are made of words, but you have too many in this sentence. "Down the street on the 13th of May in the year that Roosevelt died (Franklin, not Theodore), a spotted dog with a limp (which bespoke years of wandering, looking for the master who, oddly, disappeared the night of his high school graduation) was seen walking by a third grade teacher and her twenty-nine students."

You're tired. So what? The book midwife has been up for an hour before you got out of REM sleep. CTFU.

FOR FICTION WRITERS

Gertrude Stein said, "A Sentence is not emotional a paragraph is" (her punctuation). Readers become invested reading a paragraph, fall into the story, and take on the roles of the characters. One-sentence paragraphs make readers stop. Is the statement supposed to be pondered? Why are they stopping when they want to read the whole book? The same goes for one-word sentences, a device that messes with the rhythm necessary to keep the pages turning. Readers want to be involved in a story, taken out of their minds and into the minds of the characters. Anything that gets in the way is frustrating.

The gods have decided you need a break. This is why your PC went screwy. Dust and tidy your desk or go after the ironing. The technician will soon be there.

"I'm writing shit." Think of the Anglo-Saxon "shit" as "night soils." These were mixed with limestone, allowed to age, and used as fertilizer for plants from roses to potatoes. Night soils are our first creative act as infants, a source of income for sewage engineers, and the impetus behind engineering feats such as indoor plumbing. Without shit and the act of shitting, our bodies would become olfactory disasters. Shit is good.

Calling your stuff "shit" means your focus is sharpening and you are demanding more from the writing. Get back to work.

Being stuck means time to return the neighborhood coffee shop with your notebook. The pen is mightier than the complaint.

Poet Philip Whalen was asked, "You are hanging by your teeth from a tree branch over the Void, and someone asks, 'What is Zen?' How do you reply?" He answered, "I speak as clearly as possible with my mouth full of stones." This sums up the storyteller's job.

You're tired. Take a nap. Call back in thirty minutes, and CTFU.

TELLING A BOOK BY ITS COVER

THE COVER OF YOUR BOOK is its biggest selling point. An attractive cover will be put face out on the shelves of a brick-and-mortar bookstore, regardless of the size of the publisher or advertising dollars spent. Talk with your agent and editor and ask to be involved in the design process to check for accuracy of image and cover copy. This does not mean requesting your talented boyfriend, girlfriend, spouse, niece, or nephew be commissioned to do the artwork. Crayon is hard to reproduce with any fidelity.

Good cover copy is written in the present tense and meant as a tease. For fiction, only the main characters are described. The copy should fit the book into its genre yet stand out from the rest. Even nonfiction needs to intrigue the potential buyer. Crowding the flaps and back cover with blocks of type throws off more readers than attracts them. The right amount of text depends on the subject and audience. Be willing to make a compromise or two with your editor over cover copy. The most important part of the book remains the content, not the wrapping.

"Some day, someone ought to explain to me the theory behind dust jacket designs. I assume they are meant to catch the eye without offering any complicated problems to the mind. But they do present problems of symbolism that are too deep for me. Why is there blood on the little idol? What is the significance of the hair? Why is the iris of the eye green?

Don't answer. You probably don't know either.

RAYMOND CHANDLER, *The Long Goodbye*

If the world were a good and kind place, a reader would be convinced to pick up and buy a book only by the allure of its title. French publisher Gallimard's classic cover had a light cream color with a simple border, and the title set in red or black Bodoni or Garamond no bigger than 36 point. The reader went directly from cover to text, with no stops in between for handshakes with the writer.

In an increasingly visual world, the book as a form seems static without the ability to blink, rotate, or glow in the dark. From television to magazines to Web sites, the image attracts our eyes and the word slumps behind. Book covers must have the same vibrancy as other media elbowing into our diminished spare time. According to book-industry studies, regular book buyers make their decision in twenty-six seconds. This means the cover has to convey immediately why your book is worthy of attention.

There is no hard and fast rule for cover design: a good cover design is one that sells the book. In the 1960s, designer Merle Armitage came across a book published by the Laboratory of Anthropology in Santa Fe, New Mexico. A forbidding drab cover hid stunning color reproductions of various native artifacts of the region. In conversation with the director, he found the book was largely ignored. With a few hundred dollars in hand, Armitage designed a new cover, a colorful display of native symbols. The book sold.

Ask three booksellers (or three editors or three sales reps or three readers) "What makes an attractive book cover?" and you'll get three different responses. You should never have a pure green, a pure black, or a pure red cover. Talk to three more and you'll hear you should never have a pure purple, pure yellow, or pure gray cover. These laws hold true until a book with a pure green, black, red, purple, yellow, or gray cover hits the bestseller lists and stays there for forty-one weeks. What is important is readability. A good book cover has to pass the ten-foot test. The title should be readable from ten feet away, a bright lighthouse lamp beaming from the shelves. Any image should be simple and direct, no fussing with subtleties. The prospective buyer needs to pick up the book, and not think about picking up the book.

The cover reflects the book's themes, but not without a sense of play when the opportunity presents itself. When Penguin Books was ready to release the paperback of T. Coraghessan Boyle's *The Road to Wellville,* they wanted to do more than crank out a smaller version of the hardcover. This comic novel concerns itself with doings of a cereal / health-spa baron in Battle Creek, Michigan, home of Kellogg's Corn Flakes. The paperback was released packaged in a cereal box the same size as the book, complete with instructions on breaking the seal of the tabs and proof of purchase. Why not?

Publishers used to have separate identities, a design sensibility reflected in every book they produced. This was the result of having an in-house designer who was rigorous in defense against any esthetic improprieties. W. A. Dwiggins worked at Random House for years, where he shaped a distinctive typographic style and designed a typeface, Imprint, for book work. Jan Tschichold, the fussy German reeling from his sin of the New Typography, walked into Penguin Books in the 1930s. He gathered all the printed matter right down to purchase order forms, and gave the company a lean, classic look. His page designs remain readable and fresh. In 2005, Penguin released the *Great Ideas* series, twelve 4¼ by 7-inch books of Seneca, Thomas Paine, George Orwell, and others. The series, designed by Derek Birdsall, would have thrilled Tschichold, with covers embossed on uncoated stock and using only Sarum red and black ink. What should have been boring is exciting. The typographic arrangement jumps, dances, sings, and communicates.

After the design is completed, a coating is chosen of lay-flat laminate, press varnish, or matte finish. Lay-flat laminate insures the book a long shelf life without curling. Press varnish is a mistake, something chosen to save three cents on the unit cost, and the finished books are scuffed to unsaleability while being shipped from the printer. Matte finish is human, warm, and can be combined with a glossy spot varnish to bring out a title or a graphic for a three-dimensional look. Used alone it can scratch and show fingerprints, especially with darker colors.

Covers need imagination, and should speak to the reader, not at them. Consider the hardcover edition of Robert Pinsky's translation of *The Inferno of Dante*. The bold visual attack in silhouette of one of the damned who burns forever follows the bone of the work in a modern context. For the cover of W. S. Merwin's translation of *Purgatorio,* the detail from one of Gustav Doré's 1861 engravings gives little indication of the beauty of the translation. The content is advertised as good for you (the literary equivalent of castor oil), and the designer was down a quart on inspiration.

With the onslaught of new books published every year, your book needs the brightest dress to stand out from the unruly crowd. Too often, graphic designers who have not had access to the manuscript design the covers. This makes for confusion (see Chandler's letter). The same person who designs the interior of the book should design the exterior, so the cover reflects the interior, with the same display and text typeface. Care needs to be used in making decisions regarding images: Does the book lend itself to an image or should it be only type? The designer asks, "Who is the audience for the book, young or old, male or female, education level, specialized or general, serious or playful, product or art?"

Thomas Pynchon novels are an ecstasy for the initiated, a new land for the unsuspecting neophyte. His *Mason & Dixon* was due from Henry Holt, and the publisher wanted to make something special of its arrival. The story was about two surveyors grumbling across Pennsylvania and Maryland drawing their eponymous line in the eighteenth century. At its imposing 774 pages, the book would be a hard sell unless the cover was right. They opted for simplicity, a paper cover resembling vellum with a detail from stressed Caslon type, then wrapped in Mylar printed with the title and writer's name. After all, the story was a retelling of history through a very modern eye.

Books are fragile creatures, prone to fits of depression when stuck spine out on a brick-and-mortar bookstore shelf or left in the dark of an e-commerce warehouse. They seek readers, and a well-designed cover provides the introduction.

COUNTDOWN TO THE END

FOR FICTION AND NONFICTION WRITERS

THE EDITOR HAS sent marked-up and Post-It-laden pages and you're ready for the last round. Write a thank-you note to the editor and keep the late-night arguments, hair pulling, and rending of garments between you and the book midwife.

Amendments, additions, and queries are not mistakes. The more eyes on a manuscript the better. Not making the corrections and letting 50,000 copies go into print is a mistake.

"Deadline" means if you cross the publisher's line, you are dead. A missed deadline knocks the book's schedule out of balance. Buyers for the large chains have strict budgets and will cancel orders for any book missing its due date. They might reorder or not. The publisher, even your Uncle Ted, is completely within his rights to demand return of any advance check. Are we clear?

Rewriting ten chapters in six days is easy. The book midwife has done more in less time. Coffee and cigarettes are not Schedule One drugs. Takeout Chinese food is important, too.

Have your spouse cook and clean until you're finished, then lie and say you still have three chapters to go. Wait a month before letting him or her in on the truth. He or she should be used to the labor by then, and you can start on your next book.

Focus on the chapter in front of you, not the one ahead or behind.

When you lose a writing day or the pages you've generated are useless, the next day will be terrific, full of great energy and clear thinking. Bad days are good fuel for good days.

Writing a book is not for the meek. When the clock says 2 AM, remember you can sleep on your book tour.

Print out the chapters as they're completed. You'll feel good when you see the stacked pages.

FOR NONFICTION WRITERS

You've stiffed your editor for the extra pieces as your manuscript went through the various processes. This is the time to include everything, no excuses. Use this checklist to make sure your manuscript is complete.

MANUSCRIPT: Save as one file, not a separate file for each chapter, double-spaced, 12-point Times New Roman, with one-inch margins. All text is left aligned, not justified.

FRONT MATTER: Introduction, preface, foreword, list of illustrations, list of tables, and permissions to reprint previously published material.

FORMATTING: Set paragraph indent with ruler guides. Do not use tabs to center.

ITALIC: Forget the UNDERLINE command. Use italics to indicate italics.

CHANGES: Turn off the TRACK CHANGES and turn on ACCEPT CHANGES.

PAGE NUMBERS: Headers at the top of the page will be deleted. Page numbers belong at the bottom and in the center.

HEADS AND SUBHEADS: Put them in title case and mark the level: <A head>, <B head>, and <C head>. If your heads go below C, one of us made a mistake. Correct it.

BULLETED AND NUMBERED LISTS: Lay off the automated features. They disappear in many design programs. Keyboard the numbers and bullets manually.

HYPERLINK: Remove these from the file and italicize.

TABLES: Each should have its own separate, clearly labeled file on the disk. Indicate where they go in the manuscript with labels like <Table 1>.

ILLUSTRATIONS: Each should have its own separate, clearly labeled file on the disk. Do not paste images into the electronic manuscript. Indicate where they go with labels like <Image 1>.

FOOTNOTES: These are acceptable if there are only a few. Use endnotes instead.

BACK MATTER: Afterword, endnotes, appendices, bibliography, and reading list.

FOR FICTION AND NONFICTION WRITERS

PRINTING: If your printer doesn't have high resolution, take your disk to a service bureau. Check with your editor to make sure how he or she wants the electronic file, whether by e-mail or on a disk, and what kind he or she prefers.

Include any notes about form (whether a workbook, commonplace book, or simple straight text) in the letter of transmittal. Let your editor know likes and dislikes regarding typefaces, and mention book designs you admire. Information shared is information used.

If you've also stiffed the marketing and publicity departments on any information, such as filling out the long questionnaire, complete and send to whomever you were told. Do not include this material with the manuscript.

MAILING: Stick the manuscript and disk into an Express Mail or FedEx box. Pay the extra for insurance even though you have copies, and sip a relaxing cocktail and have a smoke. Remember these lines from a gasthaus in Oberndorf, near Salzburg: "Half of mankind is done in by alcohol and nicotine. Yet the rest, enjoying neither, does not live much longer either." Wash the glass, dump the ashtray, and start on your next book.

CHECKING THE GALLEYS

GALLEY PROOFS, OR GALLEYS, are named for the long flat ships that carried the Venetians to sack Constantinople in the thirteenth century. In traditional typography, the galley is a three-sided metal tray that holds the type as the manuscript is being set. Galleys came as long sheets before the blocks of type were arranged as pages.

Type began as *foundry type,* cast one letter at a time from lead, tin, and antimony. The letters went into a composing case and the compositors were paid according to how many inches they set each day. Compositors had to justify lines and were not above substituting a shorter or longer word regardless of the writer's intention.

Monotype followed the foundry. The compositor was at last allowed to sit and type in the manuscript at a keyboard. A paper tape with punch holes was generated and given to the caster, who fed the tape into a machine full of brass matrices and a pot of boiling metal. The type was still cast one letter at a time, except in the order of the manuscript instead of the alphabet.

The next advance came with *Linotype.* The same initial procedure as Monotype was followed until the casting. Monotype and Linotype had an argument over how the letters should come out of the machine and never spoke to each other again. Linotype set and cast the text line by line. An entire line had to reset if one letter was broken or a last-minute correction needed to be made.

Photocomposition received more threats than welcome when it became the standard. Any knowledgeable typographer can list how this upstart messed with classic typefaces and cheapened design. Photocomposition gained in popularity because it was less expensive than metal type and allowed faster composition. Galleys from this method were photocopies approximating the page layouts, usually without running heads and other extras.

Progress continued to *digital* or *desktop publishing*. With stacks of software in need of an update, and too many typefaces to choose from, all a designer needs to make a book is a keyboard, a screen, and a CPU big enough to track Verizon satellites. The galleys come as pages complete with running heads and page numbers, or e-mailed as PDF files.

Make corrections on the pages using the proofreader's marks found in *The Chicago Manual of Style* (see annotated resource list). Write corrections in the margin at the same position as the line of type you want changed. Use a pen of a color different from the editor's or proofreader's.

The manuscript has been written, rewritten, and edited. If you are compelled to rewrite the entire manuscript at this stage, refer to the part of your contract promising to pay costs over 10 percent.

In a separate pass, check heads and subheads with your original manuscript. Make sure the running heads for the chapters are correct. Add page numbers to the table of contents if not done by your editor.

A *widow* is a line of type sitting alone at the top or bottom of a page. Mark these for the designer to fix. An *orphan* is a lone word at the end of a paragraph. Read the paragraph for a word or words to delete and mark the change.

Errors creep in, and publishing companies have different standards, ranging from one mistake every fifty pages for academic publishers, to one every ten for the bottom-line commercial publishers. Read the galleys carefully.

ETHICAL COMMISERATION

FOR FICTION AND NONFICTION WRITERS

EVER SINCE ARISTOTLE puttered around the Lyceum in his second-hand toga, men and women have pondered the problem of ethics. To choose right over wrong separates us from mushroom spores and many popular snack foods. The old Greek said the virtuous enjoy doing what is right, not merely expedient, and he defined right as contributing to the Higher Good, charity, and honesty for all concerned. Humanity has evolved to consider "Is honest work overrated? Will we be caught trying to pull a fast one? If caught, how can we justify our sleazy behavior and avoid legal problems?" as the dominant questions. Answers are not forthcoming.

Big corporations own the publishing companies who put out most of the books in the United States. Shareholders demand that publishers make money above their commitment to making good books. The editorial staff is limited by time and budget, and except for scholarly works, manuscripts are rarely put through peer review. Critics of modern publishing have suggested the hiring of fact-checkers. Not a chance. Morgan Entrekin, publisher of Grove/Atlantic, hauled out his adding machine and arrived at these figures (*Publishers Weekly,* "Debating the Lessons of Frey," January 27, 2006): a fact-checker earning the low annual salary of $35,000 would read 10,000 words a week, and add about $8,750 to the production cost of a 125,000-word nonfiction book. Since this amount equals the budget for typesetting and editorial, bottom-line publishing does not allow for facts to be checked any time soon. Books guilty of plagiarism and fiction posing as memoir sneak through the system until one is caught. Apologies for the flamboyant mistakes are printed in trade publications, and business returns to normal.

Ethics in publishing is the writer's responsibility. The writer enters into an unsigned contract with the reader to be honest. This means he or she promises the book is authentic and not cribbed from another source, and every effort has been made to secure rights and permissions for quoted material. The writer also has a signed contract with the publisher, who's asking for the same, except the publisher can threaten a lawsuit if the contract is broken. An angry reader has little recourse except to shove bad books into a high-powered paper shredder and bitch online in literary weblogs.

I think I shall read. It will help me to remember that I am myself.

JOHN LE CARRÉ

Readers deserve honesty from fiction and nonfiction. If your story is worth writing, write it with integrity and respect your future reader's commitment. For the writer cursed with an eidetic memory, ask people who read too much to go through your manuscript. Slips occur even among respected historians, and having the humility to ask another to check your work will save you and your publisher professional embarrassment. Think a plot, subplot, or line of dialog in your novel sounds familiar? Rip the damn thing out right now.

No one who tries to pull a scam gets away clean. There's always someone out there who notices, and they will tell everybody down to your fifth grade English teacher. She knew you would end up in trouble.

A BRIEF GALLERY OF SINNERS AND SCHMUCKS

Clifford Irving approached McGraw-Hill in 1971 with tapes and letters from reclusive billionaire Howard Hughes, and said he was authorized to write the man's biography. McGraw-Hill and *LIFE* magazine gave him $765,000, and Irving worked with his wife,

Edith, and Richard Suskind in cobbling together forged documents. When the book was announced the following year, Hughes broke a decade-long silence and called Irving a fraud during a telephone conference. The publisher stood beside him until reporter James Phelan got hold of a set of galleys for the book. Phelan said that Irving had stolen many passages directly from his unpublished manuscript. A trial ensued and Irving pled guilty to mail fraud, forgery, conspiracy, and grand larceny. The judge and jury sentenced Irving to thirty months in jail. He served fourteen. His wife had a lesser sentence of sixty days. To prove F. Scott Fitzgerald's dictum about there being no second acts in America, after getting out of prison, Irving had to move south to Mexico and write potboilers for tortilla money. He did have a surprising third act with his book *The Hoax* (NY: Permanent Press, 1981), telling the story of the Hughes ruse. In 2006, Lasse Hallström directed a film of the same name, starring Richard Gere as Irving, and Hyperion released *The Hoax* as a paperback. Irving is too old to enjoy the money.

Harvard freshman Kaavya Viswanathan sold her first novel, *How Opal Mehta Got Kissed, Got Wild and Got a Life,* to Little, Brown and Company for $500,000 when she was seventeen. Advance copies were sent out and a movie deal was in negotiation when a careful reader spotted whole sections taken from Megan McCafferty's *Sloppy Firsts* (NY: Three Rivers Press, 2001) and *Second Helping* (NY: Three Rivers Press, 2003). Viswanathan and publisher made apologies for an honest mistake, and promised rewrites for the next printing, when another careful reader uncovered parts of *Can You Keep a Secret?* by Sophie Kinsella (NY: The Dial Press, 2004). *How Opal Mehta Got Kissed* disappeared from bookstore shelves faster than tainted aspirin, and copies are now only available for the curious on eBay. A contract for other novels was canceled along with the movie deal, and Viswanathan split the country before finishing her academic year.

A book could be written about the controversy around *A Million Little Pieces* by James Frey (NY: Doubleday, 2003), and read better than his self-aggrandizing "memoir." *Pieces* was picked as an Oprah's Book Club selection in 2005, and stickered and feted as such until *The Smoking Gun* posted on the Internet the many factual errors in the book. Frey went on *Larry King Live* and talked about emotional truth versus literal truth, and Oprah called in to offer support. Ms. Winfrey later lambasted Frey for duping readers, and he charged his agent, Kassie Evashevski, as having the idea of selling *Pieces* as a memoir instead of fiction. When demands began for a writer's note outlining the fictional elements for future printings, Frey switched the blame to Doubleday publisher Nan Talese as having made the decision to publish the work as a memoir. The fault for the controversy was with other people, not him. Frey's second memoir, *My Friend Leonard* (NY: Riverhead Books, 2005), had a different publisher, and they have since canceled the contract for two more books. A movie deal went south, but *Pieces* keeps selling in paperback. Attorneys in Washington, Illinois, and California have filed class action suits against Frey on behalf of readers wanting recompense for time wasted reading his books. Guilty verdicts are anticipated with glee.

Truth is such a rare thing, it is delightful to tell it.

EMILY DICKINSON

AFTERMATH AND WRITERS
SELLING THEIR BOOKS

FOR FICTION AND NONFICTION WRITERS

YOUR EDITOR WAS KIND ENOUGH to send a box of prepublication review copies, or pre-pubs, and they look godawful. After hitting every deadline and being the most pleasant writer the editor has worked with, your book is treated like this. The cover looks washed-out, the tables and illustrations are missing, and the paper stock is strictly discount. What happened?

Pre-pubs go out three months in advance of the *publication date,* when the book is announced to be released. Trade publications like *Publishers Weekly, Library Journal, Booklist,* and *Kirkus Reviews* need the time to schedule reviews, and they all like being treated to an extra-special preview no one else has seen.

The rough approach to pre-pubs works in their favor. Wholesalers, reviewers, and store buyers want to see the book to make a purchase or review decision. Corrections to the galleys are made after the pre-pubs are printed. There will be differences between pre-pubs and finished books, and those in the business accept this.

Pre-pubs are cranked out and shipped without proofs for the quick turnaround needed for marketing and promotion, peer review, and blurbs. The trim will be off kilter and the pages vary in printing quality. Big deal. Get them out anyway. Hold back five of your pre-pubs for sale on eBay when you hit week 63 on *The New York Times* bestseller list.

The time lag between pre-pub and finished book makes the strongest weaken. You're going through a syndrome not covered in the recent edition of the American Psychiatric Association's *Diagnostic and Statistical Manual of Mental Disorders,* the "writer-tumbling-in-a-crisis-of-inactivity" disease, caused by waiting for the advance copies of your published book. Medication helps, so do advanced surgical techniques, and bothering your fucking book midwife. Tell your spouse to stoke up the Weber and make you something nice to eat. Send leftovers.

Selling your book will not damage its integrity. Have pride in your accomplishment and tell others about the astounding new book available to them for one low price. Walt Whitman bought advertising for his *Leaves of Grass* and quoted a letter from Ralph Waldo Emerson: "I find incomparable things said incomparably well." Readers who would have missed the book sitting on the shelves of a stationer's shop were alerted to its importance and glad of the notice.

The publisher, regardless of size, is limited in what he or she can do for your book. Pushing the book is a job for the best representative of the work, who is the writer. You know every period and comma. Shyness is an error reserved for lesser mortals.

Register the title of your book as a domain name and start a Web site. Unless you're an HTML expert, have a competent professional design the site. Have hyperlinks to the publisher's Web site, and Amazon.com, Powells.com, and any other dot-com that sells books. Have a place on the site where readers can write in. Refresh the site once a month with reviews and readers' e-mails, and announce signings and public speaking events.

Compile your mailing list. This includes alumni associations and service clubs, and any organization you've paid your dues in full. They often review books by their members. Rent the mailing list of organizations involved in the same field as your book and send them fliers. If the publisher hasn't agreed to do this, visit a copy shop and crank out your own.

Many publishers generate publicity for their writers by buying ad space in the journal *Radio-TV Interview Report*. Programming directors consult this to find interesting people for their shows, and radio sells more books than television. Just ask Terry Gross at National Public Radio.

Collaborate with the publicity department so you know the show and they have copies of your book. One writer was scheduled for an early morning telephone interview with a Florida radio station. When he got on the air, his interviewer was "Bubba, the Love Sponge." The writer has been cautious about publicity ever since.

The doorbell rings. You're still in your pajamas, and smash your big toe while hopping into jeans and a shirt. Like the FedEx or UPS driver cares what you look like. They only want to drop the big box and get your signature on the electronic clipboard. You open the door, make the exchange, and use the edge of your car keys to rip into the tape on the box. The flaps pop open and there they are, fresh copies of your book.

Before joy and celebration kick in, send signed books with thank-you notes to those you mentioned in the acknowledgments. These will be offered for sale on eBay when you hit week 63 on *The New York Times* bestseller list. Send a signed copy to your editor to show you have class. Starting today you will always travel with a case or two of books, ready to press into the hands of unwary media people and also for when copies run out at a reading or signing.

Signings and *readings* are a great boost after being locked away at the keyboard. People come into the bookstore with the intention of buying your book and having you sign it. Tell everyone you know about the event, and go early and introduce yourself to the staff. At a signing, you sit at a table and sign books. Ask the person their name and write a brief note on the title page with your signature. "All the best," is simple and easy to remember, along with "Good luck" and "Hope you enjoy the read." Never write "Holiday Inn, room 327," unless they ask.

At a reading, you read from the book. Find out the allotted time and rehearse at home until you can read the excerpt smoothly without clearing your throat too often. Rehearse again. The prepared author sells more books.

On tour for *Dress Your Family in Corduroy and Denim,* David Sedaris put out a tip jar and asked people to toss in a dollar or two when he signed their books. His best night had $183 in the jar. Sedaris kept the money. With a house in Normandy and apartments in New York, Paris, and London, he's his own needy charity.

A review appears for your book, and the reviewer missed what you were saying. The fiction world is tougher. Writer A accidentally snubs Writer B at a party for Writer C, so Writer B sends out a nasty review of Writer A's new book. Writer C has to give the book a thumbs-down on account of having known Writer B longer than Writer A. When Writer A complains, he is told to have a thick skin. Writers are supposed to have thin skins to let in the stimuli for writing books. A thick skin is only good if you plan to be stuffed and mounted after death.

Being published does wear on the ego. Cowboy the fuck up. You're doing swell and the book will do better than everyone's expectations.

Since you're a published writer with a book in the marketplace, start your morning by asking what you can do to promote your work. Are there bookstores to contact for readings, listservs waiting for a notice, or fliers ready for mailing? Keep the thank-you notes going out and be nice to everyone you meet.

Your book is listed on Amazon.com and BarnesandNoble.com, and there's a nice reproduction of the cover as well. Call your friends, relatives, and acquaintances with the news. Ask them to post brief reviews online extolling the virtues of book and writer. Ex-girlfriends and ex-boyfriends are usually snotty, so forget calling them. The same goes for ex-wives and ex-husbands.

The terrible truth about publishing is that your book has three to six weeks to make its presence known. If the book hasn't sold in the numbers predicted by the marketing department, the publisher has a transient ischemic attack and forgets being involved with you or signing a contract. This goes double if you published with Uncle Ted's company. Telephone calls to Aunt Hilda begging for her intercession will not help.

Publishing is a cold business. Your editor's career hangs on sales, and too many acquisitions with low numbers will get him or her an invitation to seek employment elsewhere. The prevailing attitude is "Run with a winner, walk from a loser." Your book may have problems finding an audience. With several other books released in the same season, if yours falters, it's gone. The remaining independent brick-and-mortar bookstores clear the shelf space for bestsellers to pay the rent, and the chains have profits to earn for their shareholders. Clerks curse about the inequities and box the books for return.

Nonfiction writers should consider hiring an independent publicist. The publicist writes press releases, develops a press kit for media interviews, and arranges author tours. They work with the publisher's publicist so their efforts complement each other. Ask your agent, editor, and book midwife for recommendations. Publicists specialize in certain areas, like health, self-help, and social issues, and know where an audience is waiting for your book. Your editor will appreciate their efforts.

Writing is writing, and getting your name into the world attracts publicity, and publicity attracts book sales. Submit articles to literary journals, newspaper op-ed pages, magazines, and book reviews so you can go after the jerk who wrote the mean review of your book. When an article is accepted, ask the editor to have your byline read, "Writer A has recently published (your book title here) with (your publisher's name here)." Send copies of any articles to your editor, and in-house and independent publicist.

The book midwife promised to stick with you until the end. So I have.

Books are where things are explained to you; life is where things aren't. I'm not surprised some people prefer books. Books make sense of life. The only problem is that the lives they make sense of are other people's lives, never your own.

JULIAN BARNES, Flaubert's Parrot

ANNOTATED RESOURCE LIST

BOOKS FOR WRITERS are uneven in quality and usefulness. The best are the ones you like. Here's an opinionated list of reference and writing work.

Martha Alderson, *Blockbuster Plots Pure & Simple,* (Los Gatos, CA: Illusion Press, 2004).

For those stumbling in the dark forest of plotting, Alderson's book is a godsend. Clear instructions show how to use graphs and charts for identifying problems in fiction, along with examples from the novels of Rick Bragg, Janet Finch, Mark Twain, and Ernest J. Gaines.

Mortimer Adler and Charles Van Doren, *How to Read a Book* (NY: MJF Books, 1972).

Fusty from age and weak on literature, but the principles are solid. Read before wading into the research every book requires. Covers elementary and inspectional reading, along with fair criticism and determining a writer's message. Autodidacts will find solace here.

Judith Appelbaum, *How to Get Happily Published: A Complete and Candid Guide,* Fifth Edition (NY: HarperCollins, 1998).

Appelbaum knows what you should know. Her important reference work about the business is a fine introduction for the beginning fiction and nonfiction writer.

Diana Athill, *Stet: An Editor's Life* (NY: Grove Press, 2000).

Regarded as Britain's finest editor of fiction and nonfiction, Athill had a fifty-year career at André Deutsch, Ltd., and tells how publishing operates from the inside. Understated gossip about V.S. Naipal, Philip Roth, Jean Rhys, and others spice the pages.

Paul Auster, *Hand to Mouth: A Chronicle of Early Failure* (NY: Henry Holt, 1997).

Trying whatever came his way while pursuing the writer's profession, Auster screwed up more than most. A detective novel written under an assumed name is here, along with the baseball game he thought would make him rich. Read this instead of grousing about waiting to hear from your agent.

James Scott Bell, *Plot and Structure: Techniques and Exercises for Crafting a Plot that Grips the Reader from Start to Finish* (Cincinnati, OH: Writer's Digest Books, 2004).

Like *The Weekend Novelist,* Bell addresses the problems of plotting, using references to pop novels and movies. The exercises are strong and help identify and fix muddy plot points. Compare books and choose the one best for you.

Harold Bloom, *How to Read and* Why (NY: Scribner, 2000).

Admiration for a man who has retained his enthusiasm for the written word after years of teaching at Yale University, adds this one to the list. Reading is active, not passive, and Bloom argues its place in the Information Age.

John Boertlein, editor, *Howdunit: How Crimes are Committed and Solved* (Cincinnati, OH: Writer's Digest Books, 2001).

Do the research if a crime is committed in your story. Professionals write about the justice system, homicide, more than you want to know about autopsies, cons, sex crimes, and interrogation procedures. Learn new things and amaze your dinner guests.

R.R. Bowker, *2006 Literary Market Place* (NY: R.R. Bowker, 2006).

As the *Yellow Pages* are to local businesses, the *Literary Market*

Place, also known as the LMP, is where to go to find an agent, book packager, publisher, or publicist. Listings carry their specialties to avoid the embarrassment of sending inquiry letters for novels to publishers of bondage comic books. Save serious money by using the local library's copy.

Dorothea Brande, *Becoming a Writer* (Los Angeles, CA: J. P. Tarcher Inc., 1981).

In a reprint of the original 1934 edition, Brande focuses on developing the writer's sensibilities with chapters on learning to see, self-criticism, and the source of originality. Ignore her belief in the self-indulgent artist and take what works for you.

Robert Bringhurst, *Elements of Typographic Style 3.0* (Vancouver, BC: Hartley & Marks, 2004).

For those interested in the importance of type and page design to the finished work. Typographer and poet Bringhurst practices what he teaches, and his exacting standards have resulted in many beautiful books.

Kathryn S. Brogan, Robert Lee Brewer, and Joanna Masterson, 2006 *Guide to Literary Agents* (Cincinnati, OH: Writer's Digest Books, 2006).

This annual keeps track of over 600 agents, has a subject index for easy reference, and includes interviews with top agents Evan Marshall, Ann Rittenberg, and Donald Maass.

The Chicago Manual of Style, 15th Edition (Chicago: University of Chicago Press, 2003).

Shame on you for not having a tattered copy on your desk. This reference book answers questions about the structure of a book, uses of punctuation, how citations are noted, and manuscript preparation. A Web site for the stumped is at www.chicago manualofstyle.org.

Val Dumond, *The Elements of Nonsexist Usage* (NY: Prentice Hall Press, 1990).

Forget political correctness. Gender-specific parts of the English language confuse any writer of nonfiction who wants to be inclusive and not exclusive. This ninety-six-page book offers alternatives to the male pronoun.

Betty Edwards, *The New Drawing on the Right Side of the Brain* (NY: Jeremy P. Tarcher / Putnam, 1999).

Writers need visual acuity to describe anything from an architectural detail to a hospital emergency ward. Much of *Drawing* can be applied directly to writing, with chapters on using memory and the creative parts of your brain. Read the book, do the exercises, and the visual elements of your writing will become sharper.

Therese Eiben and Mary Gannon, *The Practical Writer: From Inspiration to Publication* (NY: Penguin Books, 2004).

Poets & Writers Magazine has created a survival kit for the writer, missing only waterproof matches. Applying for grants, choosing a title, and finding a literary community are a few of the topics covered. Smart contributors make this a real find.

Ivor H. Evans, ed., *Brewer's Dictionary of Phrase and Fable* (NY: Harper & Row, 1981).

Nothing pisses off an agent or editor more than the incorrect use of a classical allusion or slang term. Keep a copy on your desk.

Anne Fadiman, *Rereadings: Seventeen Writers Revisit Books They Love* (NY: Farrar, Straus and Giroux, 2005).

Reading is the relationship between writer and the reader as they join over the pages of a book, and rereading captures those moments. Luc Sante, Vivian Gornick, Phillip Lopate, Pico Iyer, and other hunched-over writers contribute essays on their favorite books.

John Gardner, *The Art of Fiction: Notes on Craft for Young Writers* (NY: Alfred A. Knopf, 1983); *On Becoming a Novelist* (NY: Harper & Row, 1983).

Gardner can be a pompous ass, hectoring pedant, and self-important poseur at times. In between he has brilliant things to say about writing and writers and the demands of fiction. Every serious fiction writer needs to read his books, not only the beginners addressed in the titles.

Karen Elizabeth Gordon, *The New Well-Tempered Sentence: A Punctuation Handbook for the Innocent, the Eager, and the Doomed* (NY: Ticknor & Fields, 1993); *The Deluxe Transitive Vampire: The Ultimate Handbook of Grammar for the Innocent, the Eager, and the Doomed* (NY: Pantheon Books, 1993); *The Disheveled Dictionary: A Curious Caper Through Our Sumptuous Lexicon* (NY: Houghton Mifflin, 1997).

In these kinetic volumes, Gordon feeds the English language an asphyxiating amount of nitrous oxide and transcribes the weirdness. Anyone thinking writer types are tweedy dullards needs to look at her work, and writer types need to lighten up when confused by passive sentence construction, semicolons, and the meaning of "fripperous." Gordon also knows the coolest coin laundry in Paris.

Gotham Writers' Workshop, *Writing Fiction* (NY: Bloomsbury, 2003).

Where many writing books dawdle over theories, this one goes straight to the practical with exercises and analysis. The workshop also has a school online at www.wrtitingclasses.com for those far from Manhattan, even Queens.

Stephen Halliwell, *The Poetics of Aristotle* (Chapel Hill, NC: University of North Carolina Press, 1987).

Books and courses on writing cite Aristotle's beginning, middle, and end with a lack of knowledge of what he actually said. Jump ahead and read Halliwell's translation and commentary, especially on mimesis, meaning representation or portrayal. Reading about classic dramatic forms makes for better contemporary writers.

Jonathan Kirsch, *Kirsch's Handbook of Publishing Law: For Authors, Publishers, Editors and Agents,* Second Expanded Edition (Los Angeles: Silman-James Press, 2005).

Intellectual property attorney Kirsch has updated his guide to the legal aspects of publishing. He addresses the problems with co-authors, agents, and packagers, and provides an in-depth look at the boilerplate contract. A handy reference the working writer needs for protection.

Walter Laird, *The Ballroom Dance Pack* (NY: Dorling Kindersley, 1994).

If pay attention to Jim Harrison's advice about dance before starting the writing day, at least show some class. Instructions for the waltz, quickstep, tango, rumba, samba, and cha-cha are accompanied by a CD, step cards, and feet templates.

Michael Larsen, *Literary Agents: What They Do, How They Do It, and How to Find and Work with the Right One for You* (Hoboken, NJ: John Wiley & Sons, 1996).

Larsen, an agent with Larsen–Pomada, lays out the necessity for an agent in the current publishing environment and what writers should look for. Also, he translates agency agreements and book publishing contracts into a recognized form of English.

Noah Lukeman, *The First Five Pages: A Writer's Guide to Staying Out of the Rejection Pile* (NY: Simon & Schuster, 2000).

He must be right, since his book is in print. Lukeman has been through the Manhattan publishing scene and is a literary agent to Pulitzer Prize nominees. He stresses the importance of writing clearly and shows reasons why agents and editors toss manuscripts.

Debby Mayer, *Literary Agents: The Essential Guide for Writers* (NY: Penguin Books, 1998).

More help from *Poets & Writers Magazine*. Mayer explains how agents work and the many ways of finding one for your book, and has a listing of 200 honest and forthright agents who would never think of charging a reading fee.

Stephen Blake Mettee, *How to Write a Nonfiction Book Proposal* (Clovis, CA: Quill Driver Books, 2002).

Based on Mettee's experience as publisher of Quill Driver Books, this simple guide has all the information to write a captivating proposal. Practical examples show how the pieces work together to attract the deserved fat advance. Anyone with a copy recommends this book.

Patricia T. O'Conner, *Woe is I: The Grammarphobe's Guide to Better English in Plain English* (NY: Grosset, Putnam, 1996).

A straightforward guide, kind of goofy to make it accessible, and organized for quick reference. No matter how good your high school English grades were, check this when you know you're right about a grammar question.

Flannery O'Connor, *Mystery and Manners* (NY: Farrar, Straus and Giroux, 1969).

O'Connor was asked, "Why do you write fiction?" "Because I'm good at it," she replied. *Wise Blood* and *A Good Man Is Hard to Find* prove her right. Essays begin with her devotion to peacocks and go into writing and the writer's life. Read for spark, liveliness of thought, and commitment to storytelling.

George Orwell, *Why I Write* (NY: Penguin Books, 1984).

One of the Penguin *Great Ideas* series, the copyright date is 1984 instead of 2005, as the contents are taken from a longer work, *Essays*. Marvel at the cover and page design before reading. The production is that good. Orwell has been taking slaps recently over his leftist politics not being so leftist, but his writing has a dedicated bounce many contemporary writers should envy. The title essay details his early foray into writing.

Brian R. Peterson, *The Great Duck Misunderstanding and Other Stories: The Very Best of American Fishing & Hunting Humor* (Minocqua, WI: Willow Creek Press, 2005).

Writer A asks Writer B for a quote to stick on his new book. Writer B asks, "What's in it for me? *Quid pro quo,* man." Writer A sticks Writer B's book in the resource list though it's wildly inappropriate. This is made easier by the gracefully eclectic contents of the anthology: P. J. O'Rourke, Tom Lehrer, Ted Nugent, Rich Tosches, Ian Frazier, Red Smith, and other carnivores.

Marge Piercy and Ira Wood, *So You Want to Write: How to Master the Craft of Writing Fiction and Memoir* (Wellfleet, MA: Leapfrog Press, 2005).

The pleasure starts with the frontispiece poem, "For the young who want to," and continues. Piercy and Wood are novelists who base their book on the workshops they run for aspiring writers. Basic questions on craft are answered, with exercises and examples from their writings and others'.

Robert J. Ray and Bret Norris, *The Weekend Novelist,* Revised and Updated Edition (NY: Billboard Books, 2005).

The diagrams of the turns of plot and subplots are worth the cover price, along with the exercises about developing characters. When mapping your plot, use pen and paper. The writers suggest using CorelDraw. I mean, do you want to be a computer geek or a storyteller?

Louis D. Rubin, Jr., editor, *A Writer's Companion* (NY: Harper-Collins, 1995).

Tersely covers travel, history and politics, architecture, art, popular music, literature, business, animals, science, law, philosophy, and more. Reading straight through will get you two Ph.D.s without the tuition, class schedules, and alcohol poisoning from keg parties.

Jane Smiley, *Thirteen Ways of Looking at the Novel* (NY: Alfred A. Knopf, 2005).

Smiley renews her faith in fiction and literature after the attack of September 11, 2001 and its aftermath. "…. the more novels I read, the more sensibilities I have in my head, and the greater my sense of empathy. If you have leaders who don't read novels," she told a *Los Angeles Times* interviewer, "look what big trouble you get into. They can't imagine other points of view."

Kurt Wolff, *A Portrait in Essays and Letters* (Chicago, IL: University of Chicago Press, 1991).

Founder of Pantheon Books who worked with Boris Pasternak, Günter Grass, Lou-Andreas Salomé, and Anne Morrow Lindberg writes on the publishing profession of the early half of the twentieth century. Passion, integrity, and an enthusiasm for books fill his writing. Out of print and worth searching Powells.com and Bookfinder.com.

Ben Yagoda, *The Sound on the Page: Style and Voice in Writing* (NY: HarperCollins, 2004).

Takes a Weed Whacker to the tall grass around this important and misunderstood element of telling a story. A decent range is shown in writers, too: Tobias Wolff, Michael Chabon, Camille Paglia, and Margaret Drabble among many. This will answer your questions about style if you listen.

ABOUT THE WRITER

SAL GLYNN has edited and otherwise produced more than 300 books of fiction, humor, self-help, cookery, management, social issues, memoir, and health for publishers on both coasts. He lives on an island surrounded by shark-infested waters off the coast of northern California. A strong believer in reincarnation, he was shorter in a past life. Check out www.dogwalkeddown thestreet.blogspot.com.

CREDITS

The Dog Walked Down the Street originally appeared in an abbreviated form for the Sixteenth Annual Mendocino Coast Writers Conference, August 2005, bankrolled by Cynthia Wall, LCSW.

"Telling a Book by Its Cover" was originally published in *Scorn and Wine Press,* Volume I, No. 1, May 2001, , an online journal from Colored Horse Studios (www.coloredhorse.com).

green press INITIATIVE

Cypress House is committed to preserving ancient forests and natural resources. We elected to print *The Dog Walked Down the Street* on 100% post consumer recycled paper, processed chlorine-free.

As a result, for this printing, we have saved:

7 trees (40' tall, 6-8" in diameter)

2494 gallons of water

5 million BTUs of total energy

320 pounds of solid waste

601 pounds of greenhouse gases

Cypress House made this choice because we are a member of Green Press Initiative, a nonprofit program dedicated to supporting authors, publishers, and suppliers in their efforts to reduce their use of fiber obtained from endangered forests.

For more information, visit
www.greenpressinitiative.org